T0300867

The use of consumer neuroscience in aroma marketing

The use of consumer neuroscience in aroma marketing

J. Berčík, J. Gálová and A. Pavelka

Faculty of Economics and Management
Slovak University of Agriculture in Nitra
Tr. A. Hlinku 2
94976 Nitra
Slovak Republic

Wageningen Academic
P u b l i s h e r s

EAN: 9789086863761
e-EAN: 9789086869282
ISBN: 978-90-8686-376-1
e-ISBN: 978-90-8686-928-2
DOI: 10.3920/978-90-8686-928-2

First published, 2021

© Wageningen Academic Publishers
The Netherlands, 2021

Wageningen Academic Publishers,
P.O. Box 220, 6700 AE Wageningen,
the Netherlands,
www.WageningenAcademic.com
copyright@WageningenAcademic.com

The individual contributions in this publication and any liabilities arising from them remain the responsibility of the authors.

The publisher is not responsible for possible damages, which could be a result of content derived from this publication.

This work is part of the research project APVV-17-0564 'The Use of Consumer Neuroscience and Innovative Research Solutions in Aromachology and Its Application in Production, Business and Services' and the research project VEGA 1/0570/18 'The Use of Consumer Neuroscience in the Implementation of Aromachology in Selected Sectors of the Economy', solved at the Department of Marketing and Trade, Faculty of Economics and Management, Slovak University of Agriculture in Nitra, Slovak Republic.

Book reviewers:

prof. Ing. Jana Stávková, CSc.
Department of Marketing and Trade
Faculty of Business and Economics
Mendel University in Brno
Czech Republic

dr hab. Bartłomiej Pierański, prof. UEP
Department of Commerce and Marketing
Institute of Marketing
Poznań University of Economics and Business
Poland

Table of contents

Introduction

People face countless stimuli every day, since we live in the age of information and rapid technological developments that affect every industry, and thus the consumers, too. We are exposed to an increasing number of incentives, decisions, but also stress, which all influence our preferences and emotions either consciously or unconsciously. As a result, the consumer is becoming more resilient to advertising messages, and this fact is the main driving force for the rapid, necessary, and inevitable development of marketing.

The research methods used so far in marketing have been able to provide us with rare information, but only to a certain point, while marketing researchers need even deeper information to meet the needs and expectations of consumers today. It should be noted that many of these needs and expectations are generated unknowingly, therefore cannot even be expressed by the consumer. Once marketing researchers realised the limitations of traditional research methods, they broadened their horizons and looked into neuroscience and cognitive psychology, which lead to the emergence of a new interdisciplinary science called consumer neuroscience.

Consumer neuroscience allows to survey and explore the consumer by using the tools and knowledge of neuroscience. In this case, we used electroencephalography (EEG) as one of the tools of consumer neuroscience, in order to examine the effect of aromas on consumer emotions. EEG as a neuroimaging method provided us with detailed information for choosing the right aroma to ensure effective aroma marketing in a chosen restaurant.

The research results highlighted the influence of selected aromas on the monitored emotions and enabled us to give recommendations on how to improve aromatisation in practice.

Keeping up with marketing innovations and testing these innovations can be challenging, as companies almost always have limited time and resources, therefore we suggest an effective and proven method how to provide engaging and unique experiences to customers, which at the same time informs consumers about how companies try to influence their emotions.

Chapter 1. Background

1.1 Sensory marketing and the human senses

Companies, both large and small, strive to create unique, innovative products and services that would attract the attention of consumers and hence achieve positive appreciation. Marketers are therefore trying to use sensory marketing strategies aimed at stimulating human senses, creating a better evaluation and experience. The need to engage consumer senses has gained increased attention in the last decade, and the concept of sensory marketing has emerged (*Ekebas, 2015*). On a daily basis, consumers gather a set of experiences through their senses that feed the brain, thus building an image of the world (*Tamir, 2014, as cited in Rodas-Areiza and Montoya-Restrepo, 2018*).

Human senses with consumer emotions and experiences are considered to be an important marketing paradigm and at the same time an alternative major phenomenon (*Achrol and Kotler, 2012*). Adapting to them meant that marketers had to develop marketing activities based on human emotions (*Kotler et al., 2011*). Feelings affect various parameters, including priority and choice of products or services, the time spent in the store, satisfaction with the shopping or with a product or service, consumer decision-making styles, and consumer interests and desires (*Haghigi et al., 2010*). The role of sensory experience in assessing and decision-making is therefore expressed as sensory marketing (*Hassan and Iqbal, 2016*).

The essence of sensory marketing is to have the maximum impact on the senses of customers by influencing them with various stimuli. It also should accurately and comprehensively engage the senses, evoke specific emotional responses and behaviours, which would ultimately result in higher brand awareness, stronger brand association and, of course, increased sales (*Kuczamer-Kłopotowska, 2017*).

Sensory marketing involves the consumer senses and influences their perception, judgment, and behaviour (*Krishna, 2012*). It aims to send messages to the right brain hemisphere, stimulate the senses, and ultimately create a link between the customer and the product or service and induce the purchase (*Costa et al., 2012*).

Stimuli gained through our senses go to the brain through the nervous system. Here, the brain detects and analyses them, and ultimately interprets them – this depends on past experience and beliefs. According to these interpretations, emotions and/or feelings appear that help to make decisions regarding the purchase or consumption of a particular product. After consumption, satisfaction or dissatisfaction are transferred back to the brain and help in deciding on the next purchase. In this way, the senses evoke emotions or feelings that indirectly decide on the selection or purchase of the product (*Srivastava and Singh, 2011*).

The impact of sensory marketing on the senses can be subtle, which is why consumers do not perceive them as a marketing message and do not react with the usual resistance as in the case of advertising and similar promotions. For example, *Hershey's* has long realised that the pleasure that people get when unwrapping the chocolate turns an ordinary sweet into a special experience. Another example is *Olay Regenerist* thermal skin products, designed to generate heat when applied (in spite of the fact that heat is not needed for them to be working), signalling in such a way that they are actually working. Car manufacturers have also not neglected the senses, and the 2014 *BMW M5* emitted and amplified the engine sounds through the car's sound system, even when the system was switched off. The goal was to improve the sporty feel of this car (*HBR, 2015*).

The main goal of sensory marketing is therefore to use the consumer sensory perception, in order to evoke a positive experience with the emotional connection to selected factors, such as the point of sale, brand, product, or service (*Nadányiová, 2017*).

Marketers are trying to use various information encoded by all senses to communicate with their potential target customers (*Nghiêm-Phú, 2017*).

Senses can be understood as physical means that allow to see, smell, hear, taste, and touch. For all living beings, information is gathered about the outside world as well as inside within their body through their senses, so these become extremely important. Our five main sense organs include the eyes, nose, ears, tongue, and skin (*Srivastava and Singh, 2011*).

According to *Hussain (2019)*, we recognise the following elements of sensory marketing based on human senses:
▶ the sense of sight – visual marketing;
▶ the sense of hearing – auditory marketing;
▶ the sense of smell – olfactory marketing;
▶ the sense of touch – tactile marketing;
▶ the sense of taste – gustative marketing.

Visual marketing is focused on the use of sight in marketing. Sight is still quite often considered the most important sense in marketing communication. Consumer perception is greatly influenced by general shapes, colours, design, lighting, or aesthetics, especially in the case of specific visual aspects (*Kuczamer-Kłopotowska, 2017*). Neuroscientists claim that between 50 and 80% of the processing power of our brain is devoted to seeing and processing stimuli through this sense, so its importance in marketing is understandable (*Hurt, 2012*).

Auditory marketing uses sounds and especially music. A study by *Nielsen (2015)* surveyed that almost every television commercial contained music. Given the ubiquity of music, it is essential to understand its effects, since music in advertising has been found to affect the persuasiveness of advertising by influencing mood and engagement (*Krishna et al., 2016*). In a store, unsuitable background music might send a signal to the customers that they are in a place where they do not belong. It can also affect the amount of time they spend in the store, but also customer satisfaction (*Franěk, 2007*). Thanks to the right sound system (with the right intensity, frequency, tempo, music genre, and quality), customers perceive less stress in various stressful situations related to shopping, e.g. when waiting in queues, or looking for specific goods (*Berčík and Horská, 2015*).

Research suggests that incorporating a haptic component may be beneficial for ads (*Krishna et al., 2016*). An advertising message containing a touch element is perceived as more compelling, especially when the touch helps stimulate neutral or positive sensory feedback (*Peck and Wiggins, 2006*). *Peck et al. (2013)* introduced the concept of imagining touch (haptic imaging) within marketing. Consumer research has shown that having the opportunity to touch an object evokes a stronger sense of ownership toward the particular object, thus increasing its perceived value (more in *Peck and Shu, 2009; Shu and Peck, 2011*). Touching the products positively affects buying behaviour and attitude toward purchasing (*Peck and Wiggins, 2006*).

Traditionally, the taste sense in marketing is limited to demonstrations and tastings by using demo kitchens in grocery stores, or hairdressers, opticians, and car dealers who offer coffee to their customers. In general, this sense is neglected in marketing, thus undermining the goal of creating brand awareness and building a sustainable brand image (*Hultén et al., 2009*). From a sensory point of view, researchers claim that taste physiology, an inherited trait, significantly impacts consumer tastes and preferences in the case of food and beverages (*Li et al., 2019*; more in *Hayes and Keast, 2011*, who offer an extensive literature review on this topic).

Boesveldt and de Graaf (2017) note that the chemical senses (smell and taste) play a key role in the sensory effects not only on appetite, but also food choice and intake. They are closely interconnected from a perceptual perspective. The flavour we perceive when we eat or drink is mainly a combination of smell and taste sensations, which come from the nose and mouth.

The activation of the senses is always present in the experience of consumers, and through the right delimitation of the senses as well as the right choice and evaluation of both the physical and conceptual elements to be used, it allows to contribute to the creation of unforgettable experiences (*Rodas-Areiza and Montoya-Restrepo, 2018*).

By applying sensory marketing tools, companies treat their customers confidentially, intimately, and personally, thus the ultimate objective is to emotionally connect the customers with the companies and win over their loyalty (*Rodrigues et al., 2011*).

1.2 The use of smell in marketing

In today's world, customers and consumers encounter a myriad of choices, therefore marketers are trying to find new ways how to stand out, appeal to, and eventually persuade shoppers (*Nibbe and Orth, 2017*). Some researchers and practitioners believe that due to the exhaustive use of visual and auditory stimulation (especially in the shopping environment), scents are among the few sensory tools left that might represent untapped opportunities (*Klara, 2012, as cited in Madzharov et al., 2015*).

Emsenhuber (2011) says that the advertising industry is among those businesses which are increasingly confronted with the issue of information overload. Penetrating it to reach the customer with an advertising message is therefore becoming difficult, so marketers are looking for new ways of persuading consumers to buy their products and services. Posters, newspaper advertisements, TV and radio commercials belong to the visual and auditory advertising media. These tools are, however, not sufficient and marketers are becoming focused on the use of smell.

In spite of the fact that generally not much attention is focused on scents in the environment, they cannot be avoided, and that is why they represent a potentially strong but at the same time subtle influencing factor. The unique character of human smell and the wide range of pleasant scents that are available offer a new marketing research area (*Herz, 2010; Madzharov et al., 2015*).

A scent is a sense targeting unconsciousness directly, being analysed by the brain without any consumer awareness while other senses (sight, touch, taste, or hearing) are the conscious ones (*Bradford and Desrochers, 2009*).

Vlahos (2007) states that while in the case of other senses, one thinks before reacting, in the case of smell, the brain responds before one thinks.

The use of smell is directly associated with odours. Scent is broadly defined to include various types of aromas, fragrances, perfumes, and pheromones, too. It can also be a molecule that removes molecules of odour. At the same time, it is typically a volatile chemical compound, which is carried by inhaled air and it stimulates receptors located mainly in the nose (*Scala, 2005, p. 2*). The sensation is then processed in the brain (*Schwab et al., 2008*).

Each scent is a combination of several scent molecules, therefore a large number of different combinations of scents can be perceived and recalled even at a later stage (*Hultén et al., 2009*).

This view is supported by some distinguishing features of smell, such as the fact that olfactory perception enables a certain subliminal communication ongoing between the human being and their environment, thanks to the direct connection of the olfactory system and the emotional centre (*Emsenhuber, 2011*).

Scent has generated increased attention and effort as an important aspect of sensory research (*Hultén et al., 2009; Kleinová and Vilhanová, 2013; Madzharov et al., 2015*). Olfactory information has been demonstrated to convey important sensory information that can influence the way humans interpret information in a visual-based task (Abe, 2005). Olfactory perception describes all impressions obtained by smelling. This way of perception can be linked to the various usages of scent and fragrance, whether applied on an interior architectural level (e.g. retail store, trade fairs, etc.), or on a product level such as a designed scent of a new car (*Bartholmé and Melewar, 2011*).

In the case of sight, after three months, one can remember only 50% of the things one has seen, while in the case of fragrances, this percentage can increase to 65% after one year (*Jiménez Marín and Elías Zambrano, 2018*).

The sensitivity and range of olfactory systems enables organisms to detect and discriminate between thousands of odours (Firestein, 2001). Researchers estimate that humans can remember 35% of what they smell, and the human nose can distinguish between 10,000 and one trillion different odours (*Bell, 2006; Helmenstine, 2019; Minsky, 2018*), with smell being one of the most sensitive and emotional senses.

However, the way we perceive a fragrance is changing and decreased olfactory function is very common with advancing age (*Brann and Firestein, 2014; Doty and Kamath, 2014; Mobley et al., 2014*).

A systematic review of 18 studies was undertaken by *Herz (2009)* which confirmed that there is evidence that odours can affect mood, physiology, and behaviour.

In addition, the results of a research report by *Li et al. (2007)* indicate that social preferences are subject to influences from odours at a subconscious level, whereas the availability of conscious odour information may disrupt such effects.

The smell sense is important for human experiences, memories, and well-being, too (*Hultén et al., 2009*). Scents are closely connected to our memories, they can help preserve them and allow to relive the joy of a particular place, person, or event. Despite claims that each sense evokes memories equally accurately, memories that are more emotional are evoked by scents (*Lin et al., 2018a*). This sense also has a great ability to associate certain scents with specific situations. Neuromarketing studies suggest that about 75% of emotions are associated with scents (*Bell, 2006*) and hence their effect on consumers' emotional state, which can influence their shopping and consumer behaviour (*Jiménez Marín and Elías Zambrano, 2018*).

We see that smell is widely used in marketing, it is a growing trend and presents an industry with great potential. In recent years, there has been an increase in success and innovation in this sector. In addition, many researchers are focusing on this area to better understand its workings, potential applications, and the discovery of new opportunities. Since smell is a sense that cannot be suspended, is engaged whether we are aware of it or not, and is directly tied to both our memory and emotions, it needs to be given attention (*Bradford and Desrochers, 2009*). On the other hand, scent is increasingly viewed as a communication tool for delivering a strong and complex message, and eliciting the desired response (*Brumfield, 2008*).

In the last decades, marketing scholars have examined the emotions evoked by marketing stimuli, products and brands, showing that different emotions lead to different consumption behaviour (*Calvo-Porral et al., 2019*). Scent which is accurately prepared and adjusted to customers may have an enormous impact on the atmosphere in the shop and therefore on the emotional reactions of the consumer (*Rimkute et al., 2015*).

Humans have about a thousand different olfactory receptors and each one is specialised for a particular scent (*Hultén et al., 2009*). Since the limbic system contains the keys to emotions, desires, perceptions, ideas, and imaginations, the result is immediate: when we smell a scent, we feel an emotion (*Scala, 2005, p. 6*).

In an overview of consumer studies on emotions by *Laros and Steenkamp (2005)*, the classification of emotions in positive and negative affect appears to be the most popular conceptualisation. Indeed, the primary reaction to scent is instant like or dislike (*Bosmans, 2006*). This can be attributed partly to the close link between the sense of smell and the brain's limbic part that controls the processing of emotions, as opposed to the cortex-based connections for other sensory abilities (*Lin et al., 2018a*).

Consumer research on scent has demonstrated positive effects of pleasant scents on attention and memory for brands and products as well as on information processing (*Herrmann et al., 2013; Krishna et al., 2010; Morrin and Ratneshwar, 2003; Madzharov et al., 2015*). Adding pleasant environmental olfactory cues enhances a more enjoyable environment and shopping experience and positively influences customers and visitors and their decision-making process (*Grybś-Kabocik, 2018; Mattila and Wirtz, 2001; Spangenberg et al., 1996*). It is then definitely confirmed that exposure to scent ultimately results in an increased likelihood of purchase (*Rimkute et al., 2015*).

Bradford and Desrochers (2009) introduced a framework for using scents in marketing, built up from marketer scents, product scents, and ambient scents.

The first type is *Marketer Scent*, which is used for attracting attention to selected products or services by being part of the promotional tactic (e.g. the smell of a new car in a car showroom or that of fresh pastries or coffee in a house that is currently for sale).

Next, there is *Product Scent*, where the scent is the product itself (e.g. perfumes, air fresheners, etc.). Also, small scent-dispensing devices can be purchased for homes, cars, or offices.

The last type is *Ambient Scent*, which is not emitted by a particular product, but is present in the store environment, and therefore can affect the perception of the place and the products that can be found within it, even those that have no own scent (*Gómez Ramírez et al., 2014; Parsons, 2009*). Its effect is measured by comparing customers' responses in an unscented condition with those in a scented condition (*Doucé and Janssens, 2013*).

There are two types of ambient scents which we distinguish. In the case of objective ambient scents, these are applied to affect consumer attitudes and behaviour for the retailer's benefit. *Bradford and Desrochers (2009)* argue that only this scent type is ethically acceptable because it can be recognised by the consumer. Covert objective ambient scents have been less investigated. The main difference is that they are developed to motivate or influence the behaviour below the consumer's absolute threshold of consciousness. Since the consumer does not even know that the scent is present, they cannot engage in resisting it. Also, they are not openly acknowledged or displayed, although it is not necessarily required for them to be intentionally hidden (*Martin and Smith, 2008*). Research has shown that these can influence the assessment of an object's likeability, even if the subject is not consciously aware of the scent being present in the environment (*Li et al., 2007*). The impact of pleasant ambient scents on product evaluations may be stronger than that of other affective environmental cues (*Bosmans, 2006*).

The literature discusses three functions of ambient scent – attracting attention, priming affect, and facilitating information retrieval – which trace back to the unique biological features of olfaction (*Roschk and Hosseinpour, 2020*).

Some studies suggest that the exposure to any pleasant ambient scent is enough for consumers to access particular product-related information, can cause pro-social behaviours, but also could evoke associations that enhance gambling mood (*Rimkute et al., 2015*). Ambient scents can be used in a variety of practical settings, e.g. retailers can use in-store scent diffusers, advertisers can prepare scented advertisements, package designers can use scented wrappings, and so forth (*Bosmans, 2006*). Nowadays, there is an increasing interest in the search of natural aromatic compounds because of the restrictions to the use of synthetic chemicals in foods, beverages and liquors, cosmetics, perfumes, etc. (*Lu et al., 2011*).

1.3 Scents in history

Technically, certain forms of scent marketing have always been around. Scent has been used throughout recorded history and almost every ancient civilisation has used some fragrances in one way or another, quite possibly making it one of the most ancient and automatic ways for humans to understand the world around them (*Air-Scent, 2017*).

The first scent marketers were already present in the ancient times. They were traders who sold products of a certain fragrance, such as fresh bread, fish, cheese, or flowers. The smell of these goods spread throughout the market square, thus luring people to the stands (*Emsenhuber, 2011*).

In Egypt, more than 5,000 years ago, the power of aromas was used to mask the odour of their burning victims' blood. The Romans spread scents into rooms during social events using doves. The Greeks used ceramic vessels to store fragrant essences for massaging their legendary athletes. In China, traders sold their silk using various essential oils by which they attracted their customers (*Paluchová et al., 2017*).

The world's oldest surviving perfume factory (dated back to more than 4,000 years ago) was discovered in Cyprus. Perfumery was also practiced in the Indus civilisations of India (3300 BC-1300 BC). In the 9th century, an Arab chemist published a book containing more than 100 recipes for making aromatic waters, fragrant oils and salves. By the early 13th century, the art of perfumery had spread to Western Europe, and prospered during the 16th century in Renaissance Italy and France (*Alpha Aromatics, 2018*).

In the 1920s Paris, cigarettes for women used to be sprayed with a blend of peach, jasmine, rose, patchouli, cedar, and often other fragrances to make them more attractive and sensual, being one of the earliest examples in modern times of using scents as a marketing tool (*Air-Scent, 2017*).

Clark (2009) mentions one of the first studies to highlight the importance of fragrances in the marketing industry, where in 1932 Laird conducted a test examining the relationship between product odours and consumer perceptions of their quality levels. During this research, women were exposed to four pairs of silk stockings, while each one had a certain scent of either a faint narcissus, fruit, sachet, or a natural scent that was slightly unpleasant. The results led to the conclusion that stockings smelling of narcissus were evaluated more positively, and 50% of the participating women considered them the best (*Bone and Jantrania, 1992*).

It was in the 1970s when scents began to gain recognition as a useful tool for retailers. This was at a time when the study of aromatherapy became widely accepted (*Schifferstein and Block, 2002*). Scent marketing began to be used by British supermarkets in the 1980s, when they discovered that if there was a bakery within the supermarket that spread the scent of freshly baked bread, it helped sell not only more bread, but also more of everything else, too. In 1982, there was further recognition of the importance of fragrances in the marketing industry, when the term aromachology was introduced (*Paluchová et al., 2017*).

In 1993, researchers found that scent marketing campaigns were powerful enough to increase brand loyalty as well as sales. Alan Hirsch, a Chicago-based neurologist and his colleagues conducted one of the most well-known studies within the industry, when scientists placed two identical pairs of Nike running shoes into rooms that were exactly alike, except for one difference. One room had been scented with a floral scent, while the other one was unscented. The study concluded that consumers were 84% more likely to buy the Nike running shoes in the scented room (*Girard, 2017*).

In the mid-1990s, psychologists studied the effect of fragrances on shopping behaviour and confirmed the contribution of scented sales rooms to increased sales. Hence, marketers were eager to use the olfactory communication channel as a medium for sending subliminal messages and this led to the emergence of aroma marketing (*Emsenhuber, 2011*).

While in 2016, the value of the fragrance and perfume industry was estimated at more than 40 billion dollars, it is not surprising that the global scent marketing industry was valued at 45.6 billion dollars by 2018 (*Air-Scent, 2017*).

1.4 Aromatic compounds and their impact on the consumer

A scent or odour is a volatile chemical compound that all humans and animals perceive through the sense of smell or olfaction, and is also known as an aroma or a fragrance. The type of molecule that produces an odour is called an aroma compound or an odorant. It is small, with a molecular weight of less than 300 Daltons, and can be easily dispersed in the air due to its high vapour pressure. The sense of smell can detect odours in extremely low concentrations (*Helmenstine, 2019; Alpha Aromatics, 2018*). These fragrance materials vary from very complex mixtures to single chemicals (*Soundhararajan and Kim, 2016*). Odorants are used to make perfumes, to add odour to toxic, odourless compounds (e.g. natural gas), to enhance the flavour and taste of food, and to mask undesirable scents (*Helmenstine, 2019*).

When blending scents for clients, perfumers concentrate on the 4 basic categories of aromatic sources that are used in the process of modern perfume creation. They are: plant, animal, natural, and synthetic (Table 1), while these divisions can be broken down further (Alpha Aromatics, 2018). Natural fragrances from plants and animals were mainly used until the end of the 19th century, when synthetic chemicals were introduced to the manufacture of perfume, making them more affordable to the general public. Nowadays, synthetic fragrances are increasingly used due to their advantage of constant and reproducible quality over natural fragrances (*Lange et al., 2015; Soundhararajan and Kim, 2016*).

Among the natural fragrant substances of plant origin, essential oils are the main therapeutic agents, since they represent a highly concentrated volatile and complex mixture of aromatic compounds that are obtained from different organs of the plant. There are about 17,500 aromatic plant species from different angiospermic families producing essential oils. As for fragrance components from animal origin, some of them (such as macrocyclic ketones and esters as well as aromatic nitro compounds and polycyclic aromatics – a group of musk fragrances) are also widely used in the perfume industries (*Soundhararajan and Kim, 2016*).

One of the most studied aromas is lavender and its effect on humans. Previous studies suggest that lavender contributes to mood stabilisation and has anxiolytic, sedative, analgesic, and other neuroprotective properties (*Setzer, 2009*). Also, the inhalation of lavender oil led to more active, fresher, and relaxed subjects, with higher concentrations (*Sayorwan et al., 2012*). Both the odours of orange and lavender reduced anxiety and improved mood in patients waiting for dental treatment (*Lehrner et al., 2005*). Lavender has also been shown to reduce fatigue (*Sakamoto et al., 2005*), and to increase the amount of time customers spend in a restaurant as well as the amount of purchasing (*Guéguen and Petr, 2006*). Smelling this aroma may help a seller to more easily establish a trusting negotiation to sell a car, or in a grocery

Table 1. Plant and animal sources for fragrant compounds (based on *Alpha Aromatics, 2018*).

Plant sources	Animal sources
Bark - commonly used dried barks: cinnamon, cascarilla and sassafras root; - other common bark aromatics: sandalwood, rosewood, agar wood, cedar, birch, pine and juniper	Ambergis - this sperm whale secretion is a highly prised compound due to its sweet, earthy scent; today, it is found only in synthetic form
Flowers and blossoms - rose is one of the most valuable elements; - jasmine is another pure essence; - orange flower oil, also known as neroli, and plumeria flowers are also often used, too	Civet Musk - derives from the odorous sacs of African civets; - its use is in decline due to the upsurge in synthetic musk
Resins - frankincense, labdanum, myrrh, Balsam of Peru and gum benzoin are used in natural perfumes; - pine and fir resins are preferred in synthetic scents	Castoreum - used in perfume base notes to create a leathery 'new car' smell; - it is derived from the sacs of both the North American and European Beaver, which exude this scent in order to mark their territory
Leaves and Twigs - the most popular ones are: lavender leaf, patchouli, sage, violets, rosemary and citrus	Hyraceum - a combination of musk, castoreum, civet, tobacco and agarwood; - it is derived from the petrified excrement of the African and Middle Eastern Rock Badger
Fruits - oranges, lemons and limes are the most commonly used; - grapefruit rind is utilised as well, but its synthesised form is more often preferred	Musk - it is derived from a gland of the Himalayan male musk deer; - it has been replaced by synthetic musks, sometimes referred to as 'white musk'
Roots, Rhizomes and Bulbs - iris rhizomes, vetiver roots, and several rhizomes of the ginger family are the most often utilised	
Seeds - tonka bean, carrot seed, coriander, caraway, cocoa, nutmeg, mace, cardamom and anise are used the most commonly	
Woods - sandalwood, rosewood, agarwood, birch, cedar, juniper, and pine are the most frequently used ones	

store it may induce consumers to spend more money buying products (*Sellaro et al., 2015*). Cloves (especially in the winter period) have an effect on the relaxation of respondents, too (*Berčík, 2018*).

In contrast, peppermint is an invigorating and refreshing scent that is known to increase brain activity, therefore many use it to assist with waking up or increasing energy levels. Researchers in West Virginia have revealed that people can complete exercises quicker and finish more repetitive movements in less time with the help of this stimulating scent (*Aromatech, 2017*). Evidence was found that peppermint greatly enhanced memory and alertness, too (*Moss et al., 2008*) and also a significant performance improvement was monitored in the presence of this odour (*Ho and Spence, 2005*).

The scent of cinnamon and rosemary can also increase energy and improve mental concentration. Most members of the citrus family can brighten a person's mood with their invigorating and fresh scent, including orange, lemon, lime, grapefruit, and bergamot. Lemon deserves a special mention because it is particularly effective at producing calm, clear, cheerful feelings and reducing anxiety (*Aromatech, 2018*). Ylang-ylang lengthens the speed of processing from a cognitive point of view and increases calmness (*Moss et al., 2008*). The scent of jasmine caused an increase in positive emotions, such as the feeling of well-being, and respondents felt active, fresh, and romantic (*Sayorwan et al., 2012; Sowndhararajan and Kim, 2016*). This was followed by a study of *Sowndhararajan et al. (2017)*, who also pointed out the effect of inhalation of essential oil on human brain activity.

Recognising the power of particular smells in everyday life represents an opportunity to use a fragrance as a tool to create a psychological state of mind on demand. Likewise, the memories associated with an aroma can help relive the positive feelings linked with certain people and places, and given the wide range of scents, it is possible to create a suitable scent for almost every industry (*Bergland, 2015*).

While in the past fragrances have been commonly used only in certain areas (specifically at the point-of-purchase), today aroma marketing has penetrated almost every industry. Retail stores, hotels, restaurants, grocery stores, but also senior living communities, car dealerships, and offices of every kind are diffusing aromas into the air in order to create a more positive brand experience and stimulate purchases, too. Even medical and dental offices are using aromatisation to evoke feelings of relaxation and confidence (*Batt, 2018*).

1.5 Aroma marketing and scent marketing

Aroma marketing attracts the attention of researchers as well as experts and could be defined as the utilisation of scents in order to set a particular mood, promote goods, or position a brand in the market (*Nibbe and Orth, 2017; Vlahos, 2007*). It is a method of influencing the receiver by using consciously prepared fragrance mixtures (*Morrin and Ratneshwar, 2003*) that also involves influencing the consumers at the point of sale or by the product itself (*Bartholmé and Melewar, 2011*). This type of marketing is as an effective and inventive way to market a product, or attract customers by emitting scents that would trigger positive results.

However, it represents more than just dissolving a pleasant aroma in an environment, because it is the art of taking the corporate identity, marketing messages, and target audience, then creating a smell that enhances these values (*Mravcová, 2019; Mušinská et al., 2020; Paluchová et al., 2017*).

Scent marketing in the business environment can be a vital force behind strengthening and improving brand recognition due to its power to unify a brand or product with a buyer's emotions. This type of marketing allows for the creation of an entirely new and deeper dimension in an already existing brand since it reaches the emotional triggers of targeted consumers. When sensory cues are repeated consistently, they can lead to increase in sales, traffic, time spent shopping, as well as improved brand recognition and loyalty (*Air-Scent, 2017*).

Aroma marketing providers divide their scent segments according to the location the scent is to be used at as well as the type of goods or services. The company Aroma Marketing, Ltd., in Slovakia divides its fragrances into segments as follows: Business, Automotive, Gastronomy, Stores, Relax, Entertainment, Healthcare, and Services (*Aroma Marketing, 2020*).

Retail spaces and other businesses have plenty to consider when creating the right atmosphere to suit the goods and services being sold. Location, décor, employee uniforms, lighting, air temperature, music, and increasingly smell, all these must be combined well to create an immersive brand experience (*Orvis, 2016*).

In a business environment, a scent can lead customers to choose more premium products, while at the same time retailers can easily manipulate the perception of human density. In an *electronics store*, it is essential to evoke in the customer the idea of how the appliance would be used, so in the department with kitchen appliances and coffee makers the tempting smell of coffee would work, while in the white goods section, it would be the smell of freshly washed laundry (*Aroma Marketing, 2020*).

A gas station began pumping the smell of coffee near the gas pumps and increased sales by 300% (*Serras, 2018*).

Lowe's, the second largest retailer of household goods, tools and hardware in the United States, uses the scent of freshly cut wood in its stores. It is highly unlikely to find freshly cut wood somewhere in the store, but this scent will surround customers during their time spent there and its task is to inspire to renovate homes and dive into DIY (*Orvis, 2016*).

Bloomingdales, the department store even uses different fragrances for each department, e.g. lilac in the underwear and lingerie section, the scent of baby powder for the baby clothes department, and coconut for the swimwear section (*FragranceX in Karr, 2020*).

One of Europe's largest consumer electronics retailers, *MediaMarkt*, decided to introduce scent marketing in one of their flagship stores based in the Netherlands, and just six weeks after the new bespoke scents were installed, the store registered a 40% increase in sales (*Jackson, 2018*).

Inditex, one of the most famous Spanish brands worldwide, has achieved a perfect cross-selling strategy. On the one hand, the customer is attracted to the smell of their stores and therefore spends more time in them, but customers can also buy the scent for their home with the home fragrances that the brand sells in its stores (*The Aroma Trace, 2020*).

Starbucks, one of the largest coffee shop chains, has a wooden décor with dark greens and chalkboard menus, while soft music is playing in the background, and the smell of freshly ground coffee permeates the location (*Orvis, 2016*). Interestingly, by design you do not smell the food they sell, since it conflicted with the coffee smell (*Serras, 2018*).

A Belgian bookstore decided to enhance the atmosphere of its premises with the smell of chocolate. This decision led to a 40% increase of sales of food and beverages as well as in the romantic literature section, while sales of crime stories and history books increased by 22% (*Aroma Marketing, 2017*).

The business environment can also use other benefits of aroma marketing, such as the fact that scents can also affect customers' perception of quality, the result of which is that they tend to perceive a scented product or environment as being better and would be therefore willing to pay more for their purchase (*Paluchová et al., 2017*). For example, some *high-end stores* would pump the scent of cardamom and frankincense lightly in the air to create a sense of opulence or extravagance. Furthermore, *beauty brands* that diffuse a fresh, clean scent are also perceived by consumers as high-end (*Serras, 2018*).

The olfactory journey, designed by a scent company for *the luxury mall Les Galeries Lafayette Katara Plaza* in Doha, is a composition of different trails that the visitor can follow. Each of them is in tune with the product category of the reference shopping area, such as floral Citrus scent for handbags, candy scent for eveningwear and lingerie, and soft leather for footwear. Several of the restaurant concepts have their own scents, too (e.g. in *Chocolat* in the internal zone, the ambient scent is vanilla biscuit, while *Le Jardin* with a terrace and a bar in the external zone uses a floral musky fragrance). About 70 scenting machines are installed inside the mall and controlled remotely from Italy, in order to check and adjust intensity and time-table of fragrance diffusion (*Scent Company, 2019*).

Lin et al. (2018a) provide a review of olfactory-related marketing studies, which confirm the effects of fragrances, especially in consumer behaviour. Scents can improve not only customer satisfaction, but also the evaluation of shopping venues, the effect of which can be increased consumption levels. Other important marketing variables affected when using scent include an increased brand or product recall, higher attention, haptic perception, and time spent. Of course, in order for a scent to provide these positive effects, it must be precisely prepared and adapted to customers as well as to the store (*Grybś-Kabocik, 2018*).

In addition to the already known types of fragrances, the current trend is also the development of own scents, the advantage of which is the ability to meet specific requirements, in the form of a neutralising or calming component (*Berčík, 2017*).

Many hospitality and restaurant service providers are registering fragrance and aroma of their premises as their trademark. This helps them to maintain a standard fragrance or aroma throughout their network and to create differentiation in the dining experience (*Kashyap, 2015*). The scents of popular dishes, coffee, or various delicacies that spread in the premises of gastronomic services increase the customers' desire to purchase. Thus, the aromatisation of premises can help with sales.

A pleasant aroma contributes to the overall well-being of guests and thus enhances the experience of their stay. The aroma of coffee, vanilla or basil is commonly added to restaurants. Typical for confectioneries are sweet aromas, which include cheesecake, strawberry cream, vanilla, or coffee & cake. In general, these scents evoke mainly subconscious reactions (*Wansink, 2014*).

In fact, probably the most challenging task and at the same time the most appreciated benefit of scent marketing is its ability to eliminate bad odours. Effective formulas are able to neutralise odours at a molecular level, so they not just cover up the bad smell, but completely destroy it (*Air-Scent, 2017*).

It is essential to highlight that just as scent marketing can create a positive image for a brand, so can it create a negative one. Since every person is different, they associate scents with different experiences, therefore a customer might react adversely to a brand and not even realise why. Furthermore, scent marketing can be overwhelming to some. If somebody is sensitive to smells, it may be difficult for them to spend time in a scented store. Additionally, different cultures and age groups have different associations with certain smells. What is appealing to some may be too aggressive for others (*Serras, 2018*). Therefore, it is important to choose the right type and set the right scent intensity for the relevant goods and services offered or the relevant environment (*Berčík, 2017*).

In recent years, several studies have confirmed that aroma marketing can boost sales. One of them found that when major retailers used scent marketing in their stores, the intention to make a purchase increased by up to 80%. Additionally, due to the pleasant smell in the room, customers were also encouraged to stick around longer (*Serras, 2018*).

The release of a pleasant smell within the store or restaurant has a positive effect not only on customers, but also on the employees. Pleasant odours have been found to enhance employee vigilance during tedious and lengthy tasks, even resulting in higher productivity. Pleasant odours are also more likely to improve social behaviour, which is of course beneficial when there is direct contact with people (colleagues or customers). Studies have shown that when exposed to the scent of baked cookies or roasted coffee, people are more willing to help a stranger compared to when not exposed to any smell at all (*Bowen, 2016*).

Another advantage is the ability to attract new customers. A pleasant scent can serve as a lure to those potential customers who have never been in the particular store or business before. The scent's immediate connection to the brain enables to create a first impression which is either positive or negative. In the case of establishing a positive memory, it unconsciously creates a desire to repeat it. Scent marketers generally play on this psychological fact and place great importance on the chosen scent and its power to suggest the recall of positive memories (*Air-Scent, 2017*).

A research focused on finding out how the scent affects the shopping behaviour of 325 respondents from the young generation – millennials – in Slovakia, through an anonymous questionnaire survey, where they showed a positive attitude towards aromatised spaces, and they are aware of their presence (*Kádeková et al., 2020*).

1.6 Consumer neuroscience

The application of neuromarketing techniques in the food industry has recently gained considerable popularity in both academia and commerce, evidenced by the fact that renown research companies such as Nielsen, Kantar or Ipsos have already included neuromarketing tools in their offerings (*Moya et al., 2020*).

Smells, similarly like pictures or music, have the ability to evoke memories and influence thoughts and feelings. Smells even typically operate at a subconscious level, without us noticing. However, our perceptual response to smell isn't as simple and straightforward as it is to visual or auditory stimuli (*Newson, 2017*).

Several aspects affect the consumer's decision-making and choice, including their mood, or emotional frame of mind (*Lawless and Heymann, 2010; Schiffman and Wisenblit, 2019*). Given that odours primarily have a subconscious effect, conventional marketing research methods (e.g. interviews, questionnaires, focus groups) might not reflect all relevant information and can include biases (*Berčík, 2017*). The general assumption is that human brain activity can provide more information not obtainable otherwise, researchers and marketers have thus begun to focus on the application of consumer neuroscience methods in the analysis and understanding of human behaviour in relation to marketing stimuli (*Khushaba et al., 2013*). The application of neuroimaging methods to product marketing – neuromarketing – has therefore recently gained considerable popularity (*Ariely and Berns, 2010*).

This is mainly caused by the fact that people either cannot or do not want to fully explain their decisions and preferences when explicitly asked; as human behaviour is driven by processes operating below the level of conscious awareness (*Calvert and Brammer, 2012*).

On the other hand, there are many critical aspects to the use of neuromarketing, such as privacy matters, interpretation problems, or the high costs associated with using these technologies to analyse consumer behaviour (*Fisher et al., 2010; Hensel et al., 2017; Spence et al., 2019*). Nevertheless, provided that strict protocols and methodological procedures are followed, these methods nowadays form an important part of understanding and meeting research objectives (*Feinberg et al., 2012*).

Consumer neuroscience is a relatively new interdisciplinary field that combines neuroscience, psychology, and economics in order to study how marketing strategies (and advertising) affect the brain physiologically. Within this field, consumer choice and decision-making is linked to marketing research (*Khushaba et al., 2013*).

Consumer neuroscience research applies neuroscience tools and methods to enhance better understanding of consumer behaviour, decision-making, and related processes (*Kenning and Plasmann, 2008; Plassmann et al., 2015*). A neuroscientific approach to understanding consumer behaviour has increasingly been used by business practitioners, especially consumer brand managers (*Lin et al., 2018b*). *Harris et al. (2018)* explain that consumer neuroscience research uses quantitative empirical research methods to measure non-conscious preferences and executive cognitive processes, such as decision-making. It also includes a wide range of neuroscientific and psychological research techniques to measure electrical activity of the brain and the changes in the neural metabolic activity (*Ahlert et al., 2006*) to study cognitive and affective processes (*Ciorciari, 2012*). *Harris et al. (2018)* provide a comprehensive review of all relevant neuroscience techniques with a proper explanation of their functions and utility for different types of research.

In the recent years, researchers have developed various neurophysiological methods for analysing consumer behaviour, including tools such as electroencephalography (EEG), functional magnetic resonance imaging (fMRI), and magnetoencephalography (MEG), and the growth of these methods has been made possible by technological advances (*Yadava et al., 2017*). Figure 1 shows the classification of different types of tools used in neuromarketing research, which can be divided into the ones that record metabolic activity, the ones that record electrical activity in the brain (*Bercea, 2013*), and the ones that do not record electrical activity in the brain (*Calvert et al., 2004; Cherubino et al., 2019; Kenning and Plassmann, 2005; Zurawicki, 2010*).

1.7 Electroencephalography

The brain is an extremely complex organ that provides balance and is the decision-making mechanism in the human body, since it controls each daily activity by millions of nerve cells (neurons) that communicate with each other within the brain. The electrical activity of these nerve cell groups generates EEG signals (*Yavuz and Aydemir, 2016*). Over the years, various studies have revealed that olfactory stimulation through inhalation of fragrances exerts various psychophysiological effects on human beings (*Sowndhararajan and Kim, 2016*).

EEG was first applied to humans in the 1920s by Hans Berger, a German neurologist (*Farnsworth, 2019*). EEG started to be used in consumer research studies in the early 1970s, specifically while a viewer watched television (*Krugman, 1971*) and subsequently, other researchers followed up on this study (*Alwitt, 1989; Olson and Ray, 1983; Rothschild et al., 1988*).

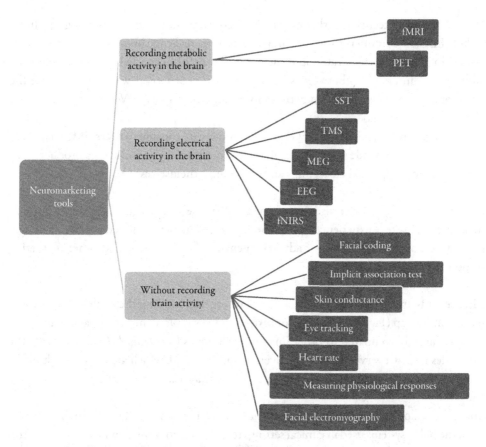

Figure 1. Classification of neuromarketing tools (based on *Bercea (2013)* and *Cherubino et al. (2019)*). EEG = electroencephalography; fMRI = functional magnetic resonance imaging; fNIRS = functional near-infrared spectroscopy; MEG = magnetoencephalography; PET = positron emission tomography; SST = steady-state topography; TMS = transcranial magnetic stimulation.

Ezzatdoost et al. (2020) points out that while decoding visual and auditory stimuli using recorded EEG signals has been commonly used in the past decades, decoding olfactory sensory input from EEG data remains a relatively new approach. Nevertheless, there are several scientists who use EEG to detect an emotional response. *Lin et al. (2018b)* provide an overview of marketing- or consumer-related EEG studies.

EEG is one of the most commonly used research methods for investigating the effect of odour on human emotions (*Berčík et al., 2016*).

The most accurate techniques that help researchers study these psychophysiological effects include EEG, since it offers the opportunity to measure real-time brain responses to various stimuli in a cost-effective, rapid and meaningful way. EEG can help to understand the multisensory interactions between smell and the other senses, as well as to measure the attentional engagement, or to study the emotive impact of a scent (*Newson, 2017*).

Neuroimaging tools (including EEG) and techniques are capable to access information in the customer's brain while generating a preference or observing a stimulus – a product (even if people cannot express their feelings and preferences themselves) (*Yadava et al., 2017*).

EEG is best used to test advertisements, movie trailers, website design and usability, app and social media, in-store experiences, print and image design, new product, packaging design, pricing, sensory studies, outdoor advertisements, political debate, and other marketing stimuli (*Cherubino et al., 2019*).

EEG records are usually taken with a device or cap surrounding the skull and electrodes placed on the cap (Figure 2). In this context, EEG is a simple, completely passive and non-invasive method compared to other imaging techniques (*Yavuz and Aydemir, 2016*). The electrodes record a very low electric current from each field, which arises as a result of the rapid movement of neurons due to nerve impulses (*Nagyová et al., 2018*).

Today, technologies are increasingly user-friendly, which is why many EEG systems have moved from the bulky systems used in clinical settings to sleek and convenient wireless systems. This allows for a range of new settings and in this form, the use of EEG has expanded. In case a research question requires a real-world scenario simulation, or if it is necessary to use EEG in combination with virtual reality software, this is already possible (*Soyyilmaz, 2021*).

EEG has several advantages compared to other imaging techniques or pure behavioural observations. The most central one is its excellent time resolution, which means it can take hundreds to thousands of snapshots of electrical activity from multiple electrodes within a single second (*iMotions, 2019*). Therefore, EEG is an ideal technology to be used for studying the precise time-course of cognitive and emotional processing underlying behaviour (*Farnsworth, 2019*).

Traditional evaluation on scent or smell product relies on trained professionals or sensory panellists, whose recruitment and training can be time-consuming, costly and may prone to subjective or subject to biases. On the other hand, EEG-based approach offers great potential in developing an objective and cost-effective tool for understanding ordinary consumer's preference in odour perception (*Zhang et al., 2017*).

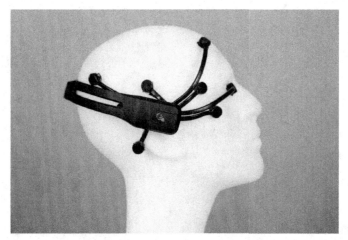

Figure 2. Emotiv EPOC EEG system.

The disadvantage of using this method is that it has poor spatial resolution compared to the fMRI (*Glaenzer, 2016*) as well as the impossibility to measure the electrical activity in the depth of the brain – the subcortical brain activity, and also the need for expert staff for results interpretation (*Nagyová et al., 2018*).

As mentioned, neuromarketing is a relatively new field of study in the marketing world, and when its tools like EEG are used correctly, it can effectively add support to traditional marketing claims. It can also aid marketers in finding the correct audience for a product as well as understanding how to market products towards the consumer more effectively (*Glaenzer, 2016*).

The Neuromarketing Science & Business Association (*NMSBA, 2020*) states that there is an increasing collaboration between science and business in research projects, proving the interest in using neuromarketing techniques in practice.

Papers and research focusing on methodological issues and technological solutions for aromachology are becoming the topics of interest in scientific journals and publications, too (for more information, see *Berčík et al., 2021a, 2021b, 2020a, 2019; Čarnogurský et al., 2021; Giacalone et al., 2021; Girona-Ruíz et al., 2021; Panovská et al., 2021*).

Chapter 2. Methodology

In order for companies to withstand the tough competitive environment, they must be able to effectively combine traditional marketing approaches with cutting-edge technologies that can provide added value and improve the overall customer experience. Aligning traditional and new approaches can be quite challenging, especially if companies do not know what these latest technologies are and how to use them to their advantage.

In this study, we point to the use of the latest technologies in the field of consumer neuroscience in combination with traditional research methods, through which it is possible to better understand the consumers and subsequently improve their experience.

The main objective was the use of electroencephalography (EEG) in monitoring the effect of aromas on consumer emotions, supplemented with monitoring the galvanic skin response (GSR) of respondents. The results of the analytical part of this publication, as well as the acquired theoretical and practical experience were used in formulating proposals and recommendations.

Within background, we provide an overview of the current state of the topic.

To develop and achieve the set goal, we followed these steps:
- obtaining and reviewing the necessary background materials related to the topic;
- selecting the research subject (restaurant) for testing the aroma under real conditions;
- guided interview with the owner of the restaurant;
- selecting 3 aromas for testing, in regards to the restaurant type, using the GroupSolver® tool;
- creating a questionnaire survey;
- addressing 22 respondents who voluntarily agreed to participate in laboratory testing;
- implementing the research (primary data collection) using EEG and GSR;
- a questionnaire survey of the opinions of the test participants on various aroma samples;
- processing the results and selecting the most suitable aroma;
- carrying out field research on the verification of the effectiveness of the aroma deployment under real conditions of the chosen restaurant and evaluating its results, formulating conclusions and proposals (Pavelka, 2017, 2019).

The research findings were processed within six subchapters.

In the first part, we described similar aroma testing using EEG, which served as inspiration for the implementation of this aroma testing.

The second part presents a selection of 3 aromas, based on the restaurant type, using the GroupSolver tool. Before carrying out testing in laboratory conditions, it was necessary to select three aromas, which would then be subjected to testing, so we launched an online survey. It contained only one question and its aim was to find out the answers to the question '*What scent do you associate a restaurant-pizzeria with*?'. The sample consisted of 100 respondents and after processing the results, GroupSolver provided us with the top 5 aromas, as well as the most common associations. Based on these results, we selected 3 aromas from the aroma portfolio of the company Aroma Marketing, Ltd., specifically Pizza Salami, Whitebread and Herbs, which belong to the gastro aromas segment.

The third part involves the collection of primary data and consists of carrying out implicit and explicit testing in laboratory conditions in order to reveal real preferences in testing the impact of selected aromas on consumer emotions. Laboratory testing took place in the Laboratory of Consumer Studies, which is located at the Faculty of Economics and Management of the Slovak University of Agriculture in Nitra (FEM SUA in Nitra), Slovak Republic. The laboratory includes a special aromatisation box (Figure 3), which offers the option to maintain constant conditions in terms of air quality, as these can greatly affect the tested aromas. The aromatisation box allows to control the amount of carbon-dioxide (CO_2), temperature, but also humidity. In addition, it allows to regulate the supply of fresh air and the extraction of exhaust air. During testing, the air temperature and humidity, as well as the amount of CO_2, were regularly checked and kept at stable levels to ensure perfect laboratory conditions: humidity at 17-18%, air temperature at 22-23 °C and the CO_2 level at 600-700 CO_2 mg/kg. These were set on the basis of the real conditions of the restaurant in which the aroma was later deployed.

Laboratory testing was carried out on a sample of 22 respondents who agreed to participate. The number of respondents was determined on the basis of similar research. *Krbot Skorić et al. (2014)* examined the effect of three aromas using the EEG in Croatia on a sample of 16 participants. *Konagai et al. (2002)* investigated the effect of soybeans aroma heated to various temperatures on EEG, where 14 healthy women aged 21-26 years were tested. EEG waves from 19 electrode sites were recorded, and the power spectrum of the alpha activity using the Fast Fourier Transform (FFT) analysis at each site was then calculated (*Nussbaumer, 1981*). In a study by *Sowndhararajan et al. (2015)*, the effect of inhalation of isomeric aroma compounds, (+)-limonene and terpinolene on human EEG activity was

Figure 3. Special aromatisation box in the Laboratory of Consumer Studies at the FEM SUA in Nitra.

evaluated by the measurement of EEG power spectrum (from 8 grounding electrodes) in 18 healthy participants. A similar research was conducted by *Ilijima et al. (2007)*, who tested 11 healthy women aged 21 or 22 in their study with normal olfactory function on the effect of grapefruit oil and neroli oil on brain responses. The commercial research of the 2muse agency (*Chovancová, 2018*) looked at the emotions evoked by different Christmas scents, on a sample of 19 respondents. The European Society for Opinion and Marketing Research (*ESOMAR, 2012*) argues that most agencies involved in market research using consumer neuroscience tools usually have much smaller sample sizes than in traditional market research, namely 15 to 30 respondents are sufficient to achieve good quality results. Neuromarketing research overlaps the limits of traditional marketing research methods because it provides more in-depth information and its great advantage is that it requires a smaller sample of respondents (15-20) than those needed for traditional methods (*Bercea, 2013*). In 2016, a similar research was carried out (*Berčík et al., 2016*) using the same EEG device, on a sample of 16 respondents.

Before the testing itself, each respondent expressed their consent by signing the following documents:

▶ Consent to biometric and neuroimaging testing, processing and storage of personal data (Table 2);

▶ Consent to taking photographs of the respondent during the research (Table 3);

▶ Training of respondents on the use of devices (Table 4).

Giving consent was followed by the preparing the respondent for testing, which consisted of putting on and calibrating the Emotiv EEG device on the respondent's head and putting the Shimmer3 GSR+ device on the respondent's fingers. An essential part of the EEG device are the felt inserts. These must be properly wetted (but not soaking wet) with saline solution first. Generally, standard multipurpose contact lens saline solution is used for this. A few drops of saline saturate the hydrator pad in the hydrator pack, thus the moisture of the felt pads is maintained when they are not in use. In case of connection problems, more saline needs to be added to each felt pad, in order to ensure good contact with the skull. After the wetting process, the sensor units with their felt pads are mounted into the black plastic headset arms, then each one is turned clockwise one-quarter until they click, which indicates they are correctly installed in a headset arm. After performing these initial installation steps, the EPOC headset can be carefully put on the respondent's head. The arms are placed

Table 2. Consent form to biometric and neuroimaging testing, processing and storage of personal data.

Consent to biometric and neuroimaging testing, processing and storage of personal data
Name and surname ....,
Address ....,
I confirm that I give my consent to the collection and processing of data through biometric methods (ECG, GSR, eye tracker, FaceReader) and the EEG neuroimaging method, as well as the management, processing and storage of my personal data and information by the Laboratory of Consumer Studies at the FEM SUA in Nitra for the needs of this research in accordance with Act no. 18/2018 on personal data protection and amending and supplementing certain Acts.
Data and information obtained through the EEG neuroimaging method will be processed and stored only for the purposes of this neuromarketing research by the Laboratory of Consumer Studies at the FEM SUA in Nitra.
The data provider declares that they are hereby duly informed about the processing and collection of their personal data.
In Nitra, on ....
....
Signature of the data provider

Table 3. Consent form to taking photographs of the respondent during the research.

Consent to taking photographs of the respondent during the research

Name and surname ....,

Address ....,

I confirm that I give my consent to taking photographs of me during the research in the Laboratory of Consumer Studies at the FEM SUA in Nitra in accordance with Act no. 18/2018 on personal data protection and amending and supplementing certain Acts.

All photographs will be processed and stored solely for the purposes of this neuromarketing research.

The data provider declares that they are hereby duly informed about the processing and acquisition of photographs.

In Nitra, on ....

....
Signature of the data provider

---

approximately as depicted in Figure 4, with the sensors with the black rubber insert just behind each ear lobe. What is essential here is the correct placement of the rubber sensor, since it is critical for correct operation (*Emotiv, 2014, p. 6-8*).

Care should also be taken to ensure that the 2 front sensors are placed approximately at the hairline or about the width of 3 fingers above the respondent's eyebrows. After the headset is in position, firstly, it is necessary to press and hold the 2 reference sensors for about 5-10 seconds. In case of good contact, the lights corresponding to the 2 reference sensors turn from red to green in the EPOC Control Panel on the computer screen. Then, each remaining sensor is pressed against the scalp until all the lights corresponding to them turn to green on the screen, too. The aim is to achieve as many green lights as possible and adjusting the position of the arms accordingly. If a sensor is not in green, other colours indicate the following status:

► black: no contact is detected (inadmissible);
► red: poor contact quality (inadmissible);
► orange, yellow: average contact quality;
► green: good contact quality.

Table 4. Signature form for training of respondents on the use of devices.

	Training of respondents on the use of devices	
	I hereby confirm that I have been trained and I am familiar with the instrumentation and devices used during testing for neuromarketing research in the Laboratory of Consumer Studies at the FEM SUA in Nitra.	
	Neuromarketing research	
	Date	
No.	**Name and surname of the respondent**	**Signature**
1.		
2.		
3.		
4.		
5.		
6.		
7.		
8.		
9.		
10.		
11.		
12.		
13.		
14.		
15.		
16.		
17.		
18.		
19.		
20.		

The device would function even with some sensor locations showing colours other than green, however, the detections would be less reliable in this state. Also, often the contact quality gradually improves after a few minutes of use (*Emotiv, 2014, p. 9-10*). Bad positioning and dry sensors are the two most common reasons for poor contact quality (*Emotiv, 2019*).

After the successful calibration of the EEG device, we proceeded to the preparation and installation of the device for measuring the galvanic skin response, which arises from the autonomous activation of the sweat glands in the skin. Sweating of the hands and feet is

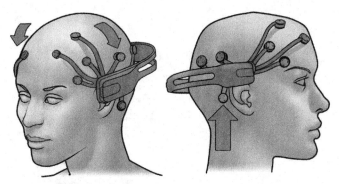

Figure 4. Headset placement on the head (*Emotiv, 2014, p. 8*).

triggered by emotional stimulation: when we are emotionally aroused, GSR data show strong patterns that are visible to the naked eye and can be statistically quantified (*iMotions, 2020*).

Before each test, we inserted the GSR device into the Consensys hardware base from Shimmer (Figure 5), which allows to easily configure it before testing and import data from the device after testing, simplifying test setup and recording data (*Shimmer, 2019a*).

GSR sensors have a surface area of 1 cm² made of Ag/AgCl (silver/silver chloride) and are placed in fastenable velcro strap electrodes, which were placed on the respondent's fingers during testing (Figure 6). To these we attached the Optical Pulse Probe – electrodes, which are connected to cables and then to the device (*Shimmer, 2018*). Subsequently, we turned on the Shimmer device by pressing the orange button and waited until the device turned green, a fact that confirms that the device began to monitor the galvanic skin response.

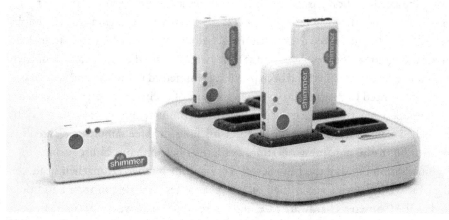

Figure 5. Shimmer Consensys hardware base (Shimmer, 2019a).

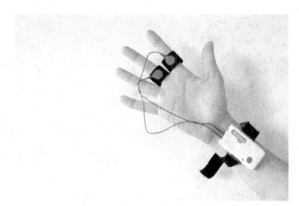

Figure 6. GSR device (Shimmer, 2019b).

After successful calibration and deployment of the EEG and GSR devices, the respondent moved to the aromatisation box and was instructed on how the testing would proceed. In this box, on the left side of the rack, samples of aromas were placed in similarly looking containers and numbered 1, 2 and 3. There was also a tablet computer in the box, on which the questionnaire was displayed (Table 5). In addition to the aromas, the respondent had alcohol available as a neutraliser that they could smell between the samples. The role of alcohol was to restart the respondent's olfactory senses so that they could continue testing the other samples. Sensory interruption between two sensory-rich stimuli clears the trace of the earlier sensory cue and enhances the sensitivity of the later one (*Biswas et al., 2014*). Research has shown that e.g. smelling coffee beans between sampling scent strips acts as a form of sensory interruption, too, because it works for cleansing the nasal palate after each fragrance evaluation (*Cleary et al., 2010; Secundo and Sobel, 2006*).

After closing the aromatisation box, the respondent continued to receive instructions through a transmitter. The respondent was instructed on exactly when to start smelling which sample, and after each one, they answered the question that belonged to that particular sample. We changed the order of the samples so that no samples were favoured or disadvantaged. Each sample contained filter paper that had been previously immersed in the selected aroma, and the sample was scented by respondents 3-10 cm in front of their nose. Respondents had a 2-minute break between testing each scent to reduce or eliminate the effect of the previous one and smelled alcohol during that break. After smelling all three samples, we asked the respondent to fill in the remaining questions from the questionnaire. Subsequently, they left the aromatisation box and the EEG device was carefully removed from their head, the recording of the GSR device was turned off, the electrodes were disconnected and then connected to the Consensys hardware base, and the recorded data was imported.

Table 5. Questionnaire form designed for testing in laboratory conditions.

Questionnaire designed for testing in laboratory conditions

Evaluation of aromas in laboratory conditions

Dear respondent,

We are conducting a research on the effect of aromas on consumer emotions. For this reason, we are asking for a few minutes of your attention to complete this questionnaire. The questionnaire is anonymous and all data provided by you will be used exclusively for the purposes of this research. Thank you for your time and cooperation.

1) How do you evaluate Scent 1?	4) Gender
▸ Very pleasant	▸ Female
▸ Pleasant	▸ Male
▸ Neutral	5) Age
▸ Unpleasant	▸ Under 25 years
▸ Very unpleasant	▸ 26-35 years
2) How do you evaluate Scent 2?	▸ 36-45 years
▸ Very pleasant	▸ 46-55 years
▸ Pleasant	▸ 56 years or older
▸ Neutral	6) Employment status
▸ Unpleasant	▸ Student
▸ Very unpleasant	▸ Employed / Self-employed
3) How do you evaluate Scent 3?	▸ Unemployed
▸ Very pleasant	▸ Retired
▸ Pleasant	▸ Other ....
▸ Neutral	7) How are you feeling today?
▸ Unpleasant	▸ ....
▸ Very unpleasant	

Explicit testing consisted of completing a questionnaire, which was created using the Google Forms application, a tool designed specifically for the creation of online questionnaires, collection and evaluation of respondents' answers. The questionnaire consisted of 2 parts and 7 questions. The first part included the first 3 questions, which were focused on the evaluation of the three selected aromas and the second part continued with three demographic questions and one open one asking about the mood of the respondents. The main task of the survey was to find out the respondents' opinions on the tested samples, as well as gather data with which we would then be able to characterise the respondents. With the questionnaire, we verified the results obtained by biometric and neuroimaging methods and then we compared the conscious and unconscious perception of the given aromas for the respondents.

Next, the fourth part of the research findings describes the evaluation of laboratory testing, which consisted of mathematical-statistical processing. For each aroma, we monitored the 10-second interval immediately after smelling, and the Mind Your OSCs software provided us with the values of particular emotions for each monitored second. We processed these values using descriptive statistics. The nature of the data from the questionnaire allowed us to examine whether there was a statistically significant difference in the evaluation of each scent, and we performed this examination using the Friedman test. Furthermore, we also used Chi-Square Test of Independence, in order to find out whether there is a statistically significant difference between men and women in the evaluation of these scents.

Consequently, the fifth part is focused on verifying the effectiveness of aromatic compounds by their deployment under real conditions of the restaurant, while the periods without and with aromatisation were monitored. Testing under real conditions took place in a restaurant, located in the centre of the village of Ludanice in Slovakia. The aromatised space has an area of approximately 72 m², so we chose to use the AromaStreamer® 650 Bluetooth scent machine. The compact device (Figure 7) works with the principle of smooth and micro fine nebulisation (dispersion) of exclusive perfume compositions, which guarantees a quick aromatisation of areas up to 150 m². Thanks to the built-in multifunction timer, the device can be easily accessed by an app via Bluetooth and quickly programmed to the desired working hours. Scenting intervals are programmable to the second and guarantee a uniform and optimal scenting effect. Unpleasant odours are removed quickly and effectively by an absorber (neutralising substance) found in the scents. The chosen scent machine measures 26 × 21 × 9 cm and weighs 3,150 g, so it does not take up much space in the restaurant and it discreetly scents (*REIMA AirConcept, 2019*).

Figure 7. AromaStreamer® 650 (Aroma Marketing, 2021).

The scent machine can be set up through an app (REIMA App), which can be downloaded free of charge from the App Store or Google Play Store, for smartphones running on Android and iOS operating systems. AromaStreamer 650 works via Bluetooth, so it is necessary to activate Bluetooth on the phone before launching the application. The app displays scent machines that are located nearby, the one to be set is chosen, a password is entered and the device name can be changed, if necessary.

We set our scent machine for 2 weeks, Monday to Sunday, with an intensity of 15. The restaurant's opening hours are from 10:00 to 22:00, so aromatisation started at 9:30 in order to have the room properly aromatised by its opening, until the closing time of the restaurant.

Lastly, the sixth part consisted of the evaluation of the survey under real conditions (Table 6) in order to verify the conscious feedback. The questionnaire survey contained 3 questions, with which we tried to find out whether customers perceive the scent in the room and how they evaluate it, complemented with a demographic question.

Table 6. Questionnaire form designed for testing under real conditions.

Questionnaire designed for testing under real conditions
Evaluation of aromas under real conditions
Dear respondent,
We are conducting a research on the effect of aromas on consumer emotions. For this reason, we are asking for a few minutes of your attention to complete this questionnaire. The questionnaire is anonymous and all data provided by you will be used exclusively for the purposes of this research. Thank you for your time and cooperation.
1) Have you perceived that the restaurant is aromatised?
▸ Yes
▸ No
2) If yes, what do you think about the scent?
▸ Very pleasant
▸ Pleasant
▸ Neutral
▸ Unpleasant
▸ Very unpleasant
3) Gender
▸ Female
▸ Male

In this publication, we used the following methods of data collection:

- An association test using GroupSolver (*2021a, 2021b*). Data was collected from respondents' answers to open-ended questions. GroupSolver is a branded tool that blends machine learning with crowd intelligence (both filter out noise and duplicate answers in real-time) and advanced statistics. It cleans, organises and quantifies natural text answers in real-time, and it provides a dynamic and self-calibrating algorithm to quantify the qualitative insights.
- Measuring implicit feedback through monitoring electrical activity and brain waves using the Emotiv EPOC portable 14-channel EEG system (*Emotiv, 2020*), which records electrical activity through 14 biopotential sensors placed on the scalp, each representing a channel. It works via Bluetooth, enabling immediate transmission and processing of recorded data, over the 2.4 GHz band (*Emotiv, 2014*).
- The EPOC headset has two electrode arms each containing 9 locations with 7 data collecting sensors and 2 references (*Emotiv, 2019*), which are placed and marked in compliance with the international 10-20 system of electrode placement (*Nuwer et al., 1998*). The system is based on the distances between adjacent electrodes, which are either 10% or 20% of the total front-back or right-left distance of the skull (*TCT, 2012*). Following the international norms of the American Electroencephalographic Society (*AES, 1994*) in available places were: AF3, F7, F3, FC5, T7, P7, O1, O2, P8, T8, FC6, F4, F8 and AF4. The validation of the mobile EEG device from Emotiv EPOC was verified by researchers such as *Badcock et al. (2013), Duvinage et al. (2013) and Hairston et al. (2014)*, who used this device for surveying the emotional state of respondents in motion, while results indicated that the device provides almost the same results as traditional stationary EEG.
- Raw data obtained by electroencephalography was cleared of disturbing artefacts, transformed, and then classified into emotions through the open-access platform OpenViBE v2.2.0, which allows the creation of a real-time data processing algorithm. EEG signals in the alpha (7-13 Hz) and beta zones (13-30 Hz) are in the centre of focus when researching the emotional valence, frustration, excitement and engagement (*Ramirez and Vamvakousis, 2012*).
- We monitored four basic emotional states: excitement, meditation, frustration, and emotional engagement. The most discriminative variables for this model were selected based on previous studies by *Berka et al. (2007), Coelli et al. (2015) and Stikic et al. (2014)* using stepwise regression. Excitement was calculated based on *Giraldo and Ramirez (2013)*, also used in a study by *McMahan et al. (2015)*. While no studies have yet investigated EEG-based frustration detection, some have elucidated the roles of the prefrontal cortex and the parietal lobe in frustration (*Abler et al., 2005; Deveney et al., 2013; Rich et al., 2010*), lending credibility to our observations.

- ▶ Monitoring the galvanic skin response using a mobile Shimmer3 GSR+, which records the electro-dermal activity (or skin resistance) of the skin non-invasively between two reusable electrodes attached to two fingers of one hand. In response to stimuli, sweat glands become more active, increasing moisture content on the skin, hence increasing skin conductance and thus decreasing skin resistance (*Shimmer, 2018*).
- ▶ Guided interview with the restaurant owner.
- ▶ Using a questionnaire survey, both in laboratory research and in testing under real conditions. Using this survey, we found out opinions and facts, based on pre-designed questions. The task of the respondents was to record data that represented the answers for a structured set of questions.

The methods used to process the data were as follows:
- ▶ Statistical processing in the Emotiv EPOC Control Panel 1.0.0.5-PREMIUM software, which measures and displays a wide range of subjective emotional reactions that the respondent experiences in real time. Levels of engagement, frustration, meditation, excitement, and long-term excitement are reflected in graphical measurements on control panel dials (*Emotiv, 2014*).
- ▶ Mind Your OSCs software, also from Emotiv, which displays real-time values of particular emotions via a universal score from 0 to 1.
- ▶ Statistical processing using the Consensus Solution™ from GroupSolver, which presents a grouping of ideas that the largest number of respondents would agree with. The tool's algorithm builds a consensus based on frequency of overlap, statistical significance, and overall idea support (*GroupSolver, 2020*).
- ▶ Contingency tables, used for a tabular representation of categorical data. It usually shows frequencies for particular combinations of values of two discrete random variable s X and Y, while each cell in the table represents a mutually exclusive combination of X-Y values (*Statistics, 2020*).

Data obtained using the EEG neuroimaging method, the GSR biometric method and the traditional questionnaire were subsequently processed by mathematical and statistical methods – descriptive statistics such as arithmetic mean and median, and inductive statistics such as Friedman Test and Chi-Square Test of Independence (*Statistics Solutions, 2019*).

Chapter 3. Research findings

In the highly competitive environment of the 21st century, most companies use only two of the five senses (sight and hearing) in their marketing strategies. However, emotions are closely linked to the sense of smell, so it is not surprising that companies which are open to new possibilities have gradually recognised that building emotional bonds between consumers and products using scents is crucial.

Several studies have already confirmed that the use of aromas can have a significant and direct impact on business profitability, which is why their use should be a key part of the marketing strategy. Research has focused on examining the impact of different scents on consumers, so that these findings can then be put into practice. Aroma research can be carried out with several tools, both traditional, such as a questionnaire, but also new ones, such as EEG.

Researches on this topic include one carried out in Croatia, where they decided to monitor and analyse the human brain activity while perceiving 3 scents (lemon, peppermint and vanilla) with an EEG device. The research was carried out on a sample of 16 respondents who were seated in a sound- and light-insulated chamber with its own ventilation system and gradually smelled the selected scents, in random order. The results showed that the smell of peppermint and lemon caused a statistically significant difference in the intensity of brain activity between different areas, whereas vanilla was not statistically proven. Since vanilla had the least effect and respondents described it as very mild, we can assume that vanilla did not have the same effect on the olfactory system as the other two fragrances. All the scents were rated as pleasant, which is also important because the degree of pleasantness affects the intensity of brain activity and it is also possible to classify EEG signals to determine whether the smell is perceived as pleasant or unpleasant (*Krbot Skorić et al., 2014*).

Based on the above research, as well as information from other researches in this area, we decided to conduct a similar research and chose electroencephalography as a tool to monitor the impact of aromas on consumer emotions. In order to obtain more in-depth information, we supplemented the results of electroencephalography (EEG) with a biometric research method, namely galvanic skin response (GSR) and we also used a traditional questionnaire. After completing the laboratory testing and processing the results, we continued our research with testing under real conditions.

The research was relatively comprehensive, as it included testing in laboratory conditions, using several testing methods, as well as testing of obtained information under real conditions.

The chosen object of the study, the restaurant (Figure 8), offers quality cuisine for more than 20 years, with a variety of dishes on its menu, but pizza is the basis, currently with a choice of 25 types.

The success of the restaurant is evidenced not only by its long presence on the market and satisfied customers, but also by financial indicators, such as sales (Figure 9). The restaurant's sales have been growing over the last 5 years and they have seen the strongest growth in the last 3 years.

Figure 8. Premises of the restaurant.

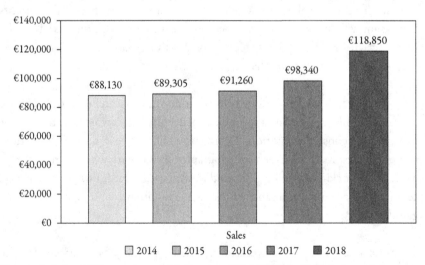

Figure 9. Sales of the restaurant between 2014-2018 in EUR (Internal documents of the company, 2019).

Another indicator is the number of employees, which in the last 5 years ranged between 4-6 permanent employees and 2-3 part-time workers during the summer season. Overall, the chosen restaurant is successful, but the owner herself realises that in order for this success to persist, it is necessary to introduce innovative solutions, such as aroma marketing.

3.1 Selection of aromas for laboratory research

Laboratory research was preceded by the selection of 3 aromas to be tested. The selection of these aromas was made on the basis of the results of the GroupSolver tool, which processed the answers of respondents from the online environment to the question *'What scent do you associate a smell of a restaurant-pizzeria with?'*. GroupSolver provided us with an output (Figure 10) with the top 5 scents that respondents associate with this restaurant type (a pizzeria), which included basil, spices, tomatoes, cheese and baked dough. The output also provided us with a grouping of ideas with which the largest number of respondents agree, for example 'Basil, garlic, baked dough, cheese reminds me of a pizzeria' or 'Baking, spices, food', etc.

Based on these results, we chose aromas from the gastro segment offered by Aroma Marketing, Ltd., specifically Pizza Salami, Whitebread and Herbs to be dispersed within the restaurant. The first aroma, Pizza Salami, was created to evoke a spicy aroma of freshly baked pizza, with salami and grated cheese in consumer minds. This scent has within its composition several aromas of our top 5, both spices, baked dough, but also cheese, while the grouping of ideas we see in the output also contains these types of scents. The Whitebread aroma represents a sweet and pleasant aroma of white bread, and since there is baked dough in the top 5 aroma classification, we decided to test this one as well. The last scent, Herbs, is reminiscent of an aromatic and tasty mixture of herbs and spices. Basil and spices took first

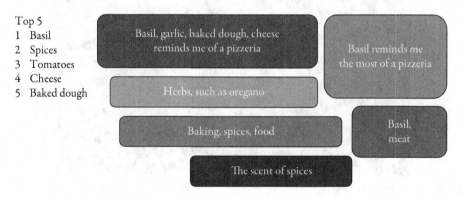

Figure 10. GroupSolver results.

and second place in the top 5, and also in the grouping of ideas, we see that basil and spices were often repeated, one of the answers even says that the smell of basil is probably most associated with a pizzeria, so the choice of Herbs was certain.

3.2 Research under laboratory conditions

We examined the effect of scents on consumer emotions only after a guided interview with the restaurant owner, selection of three aromas and preparation of all necessary documents. The laboratory research took place in the Laboratory of Consumer Studies at the FEM SUA in Nitra, Slovakia. This laboratory includes an aromatisation box, in which the respondents tested the samples, and a control room from where we managed the research.

The chosen 3 scents were presented to the respondents in numbered samplers (Figure 11). These samples contained a piece of filter paper that had previously been immersed in the selected aroma. Sample number 1 was Pizza Salami, sample number 2 was Whitebread and sample number 3 was Herbs.

Our research involved 22 respondents, who first provided some demographic information in the questionnaire. The gender structure of the respondents was perfectly balanced, 50% were female and 50% male. In the age structure, the first age group of respondents (under 25 years) had the largest representation (68.18%), while the category between 26 years to 35 years was 13.64%. In terms of current economic status of respondents, 68.18% were students, 27.27% employees or self-employed and 4.55% were pensioners (Table 7 for details on demographic characteristics).

Figure 11. Scent samples.

Table 7. Demographic characteristics of respondents.

Gender	Absolute frequency	Relative frequency
Male	11	50.00%
Female	11	50.00%
Total	22	100.00%
Age	**Absolute frequency**	**Relative frequency**
Under 25 years	15	68.18%
26-35 years	3	13.64%
36-45 years	2	9.09%
46-55 years	0	0.00%
56 years or older	2	9.09%
Total	22	100.00%
Employment status	**Absolute frequency**	**Relative frequency**
Student	15	68.18%
Employed / Self-employed	6	27.27%
Unemployed	0	0.00%
Retired	1	4.55%
Other	0	0.00%
Total	22	100.00%
Gender	**Absolute frequency**	**Relative frequency**
Female	21	36.84%
Male	36	63.16%
Total	57	100.00%

Each respondent tested each scent and their electrical activity and brainwaves were monitored by a neuroimaging method, using the Emotiv EPOC mobile EEG device. At the same time, we also monitored the galvanic skin response with a biometric method, namely the mobile Shimmer3 GSR+. Before the testing itself, it was necessary to calibrate each respondent, and only after a successful calibration could the respondent be moved to the aromatisation box and consequently testing could take place (Figure 12).

During the testing process, the respondent received instructions on when to start smelling which sample and from the control room of the laboratory we recorded data and monitored the course of emotions (Figure 13). The EEG data were transferred to the Emotiv Control Panel 1.0.0.5-PREMIUM software, which processed them and then graphically displayed the course of emotions that the respondent experienced in real time, while the Mind Your OSCs software, also from Emotiv, displayed in real time the values of particular emotions through a universal score from 0 to 1.

Figure 12. Scent testing.

Figure 13. The testing process analysed by software.

We monitored our respondents' engagement, meditation, frustration, immediate excitement, and long-term excitement. Recording engagement allows to examine their oversight, alertness, concentration, stimulation, and interest, while in case of immediate excitement it is about excitement, nervousness and unrest. Frustration allows to examine this exact emotion. Detection of meditation represents the level of relaxation or stress. These emotions take values or scores from 0 to 1, where 0 represents the absence of the emotion and 1 a strong presence, but in the case of meditation, values approaching 1 indicate mental relaxation, while 0 represents stress or discomfort (*Harris, 2017*).

For each emotion, we observed a 10-second interval right after smelling. We then processed the values of each emotion within this interval using descriptive statistics (Table 8). The highest values were recorded for scent 3 (Herbs), where during the first four seconds, we recorded values above 0.6. On the other hand, we recorded the smallest values for scent 1 (Pizza Salami), where the engagement values did not exceed 0.556. We did not notice a significant increase or decrease for scent 2, so the course was relatively constant.

Next, we examined the score of each scent based on average values (Figure 14). It is notable that scent 3 achieved the highest score of 0.598, so the presence of this emotion in the respondents was not negligible. Scent 2 had an average score of 0.568 and scent 1 had a score of 0.548. There are relatively high differences between these scents, because in EEG measurements, even a small change in value indicates a large change in the respondent's brain activity.

We know that scent 3 resembles an aromatic mixture of herbs and spices. In gastronomy, both are irreplaceable because they stimulate our taste buds and at the same time affect other senses, such as smell and even eyesight. A small amount of various spices can completely change the taste of food, because they are highly concentrated and stimulating. Given this information, it is possible that scent 3 received the highest score, because the aromatic mixture of herbs and spices has a stimulating effect and this stimulation is directly related to engagement.

Table 8. Time course of engagement.

Second / Scent	1	2	3	4	5	6	7	8	9	10
Scent 1	0.556	0.555	0.553	0.549	0.546	0.545	0.547	0.547	0.546	0.544
Scent 2	0.570	0.566	0.566	0.567	0.570	0.570	0.571	0.571	0.570	0.567
Scent 3	0.619	0.617	0.613	0.603	0.592	0.587	0.586	0.585	0.590	0.593

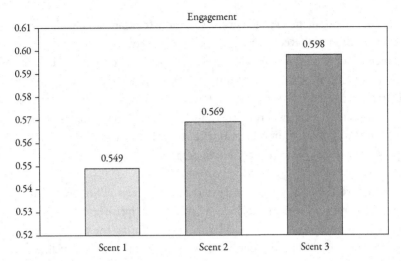

Figure 14. Score for engagement.

In the next stage, we proceeded to evaluate the emotion Frustration (Table 9). Scent 1 had the lowest values of all three, its highest recorded value was only 0.462. On the other hand, scent 2 had the highest values during all 10 seconds. The lowest recorded value for scent 2 was 0.492, while the highest was 0.517, so we see that there is a relatively large difference between these two aromas. Scent 3 values ranged from 0.474 to 0.506. In the case of scents 2 and 3, a more pronounced increase occurred in the fifth second and the increasing tendency lasted for up to 8 seconds and 9 seconds, respectively.

A graphical representation of the scores achieved (Figure 15) shows that scent 2 caused the highest level of frustration. We assume that this was due to the fact that the respondents had difficulties identifying the smell, as it is perceived softer than the others and not everyone could identify it immediately, thus this could have caused frustration. After testing, several respondents asked what aroma was present in sample 2.

Table 9. Time course of frustration.

Second / Scent	1	2	3	4	5	6	7	8	9	10
Scent 1	0.451	0.460	**0.462**	0.460	0.457	0.454	0.459	0.454	0.452	0.458
Scent 2	**0.492**	0.498	0.496	0.496	0.506	0.510	0.510	0.508	0.508	**0.517**
Scent 3	0.474	0.480	0.482	0.482	0.489	0.497	0.502	0.506	0.504	0.502

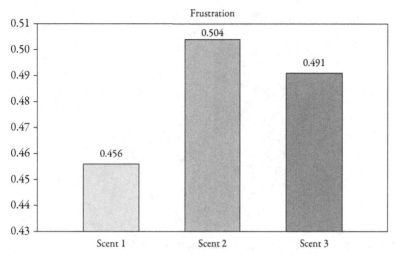

Figure 15. Score for frustration.

As already mentioned, scent 3 represents a mixture of different herbs and spices, so even in this case it is possible that the respondents tried to specifically identify which herbs and spices they felt when smelling this sample. Given that frustration is rather a negative emotion that we do not want to evoke in consumers, we evaluate scent 1 as the best, since it has the lowest values of this emotion.

On the other hand, when we look at the conscious evaluation of scent 1 through the laboratory questionnaire, we see that scent 1 was rated the most negative. Figure 16 shows the answers to the first question of the questionnaire ('How do you evaluate Scent 1?'). Possible answers included five options: very pleasant, pleasant, neutral, unpleasant and very unpleasant. In this question, 45% of respondents marked unpleasant and 27% very unpleasant as the answer. 23% of respondents rated it as neutral and 5% rated it as pleasant, while no one considered the smell being very pleasant.

Certainly, conscious negative evaluation of a scent through the questionnaire is not the only factor of the high degree of frustration, but when the respondent evaluates the smell as unpleasant or even very unpleasant, they probably express that either the smell reminded them of a negative memory, identified some component that negatively affects them or possibly they could not identify the smell itself or what they liked or did not like in it, and in such cases, a stronger presence of frustration is usually expected, which was not proven in our case.

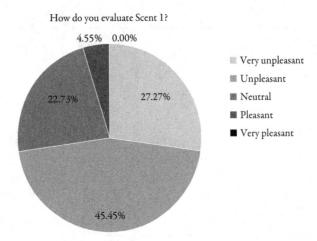

Figure 16. Response to the first question in laboratory conditions.

Another emotion we observed was meditation (Table 10). Overall, for all 3 scents, the values of meditation were lower than for other emotions, but on the other hand, we noticed a more significant increase and decrease for each scent. In the case of meditation, the closer the values are to 1, the stronger the presence of mental relaxation, and the closer the values are to 0, the stronger the presence of stress. The measured values for all scents are closer to 0, so the respondents showed stress rather than mental relaxation. We recorded the highest values for scent 2, here the highest one being 0.373 in the fifth second. Scent 1 had the lowest values during the entire period of 10 seconds, where the highest value reached only 0.343 in the ninth and tenth second and the lowest value was 0.335 in the second and third second. Scent 2 had a relatively fluctuating course, as the values changed more significantly from one second to the next. For example, for this scent, the meditation level was 0.352 in the fourth second, while in the fifth it rose to 0.373 and fell again to 0.354 in the sixth second.

In the graphical representation (Figure 17), we also see that scent 2 had the highest score (0.350) and scent 1 had the lowest one (0.339). We state that the score of all 3 scents was close to 0, but scent 2 had the highest value, so we evaluate this the most positively of the selected three.

Table 10. Time course of meditation.

Second / Scent	1	2	3	4	5	6	7	8	9	10
Scent 1	0.340	**0.335**	**0.335**	0.339	0.340	0.340	0.337	0.340	**0.343**	**0.343**
Scent 2	0.332	0.340	0.345	0.352	**0.373**	0.354	0.354	0.349	0.348	0.357
Scent 3	0.349	0.353	0.357	0.354	0.350	0.346	0.340	0.340	0.345	0.346

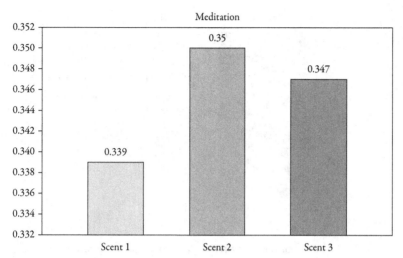

Figure 17. Score for meditation.

The aromas we have selected for laboratory testing belong to the gastro aromas segment, so they simulate the smell of a certain food and their task is to arouse interest in this type of food, or to evoke an immediate appetite, thus the measured values do not approach 1. Aromas were created to lead to an act, such as ordering and consuming a certain type of food or drink, rather than creating a profound subconscious influence.

Based on the answers provided in the questionnaire (Figure 18), up to 50% of respondents described scent 2 as unpleasant, 23% marked it as neutral, 14% as pleasant and 9% as very unpleasant. No respondent rated this scent as very pleasant. When comparing the results of conscious and unconscious evaluation, it is possible that the recorded low level of meditation was caused by a negative subconscious influence, which led the respondents to evaluate the given scent negatively.

Excitement as a state of arousal is an important emotion in consumers. When a person is excited, they also experience other types of emotions more intensely and it can affect their decision-making process, too. Excited consumers are more likely to make a decision – even a bad one, because excitement leads to impulsivity (*Patel, 2021*). During the observed period of time, scent 3 evoked the highest level of excitement (Table 11). Except for the first second and the last two, in all other times the excitement value was above 0.7, demonstrating the high presence of this emotion in the respondents. Scent 2 also evoked this emotion, but the highest value was lower at 0.623. Scent 1 had the least effect because the recorded values were smaller than for the other two aromas (the highest value recorded was 0.523). The course of excitement was relatively constant for the observed scents, while more significant changes were recorded in the last 4 seconds only in the case of scent 2.

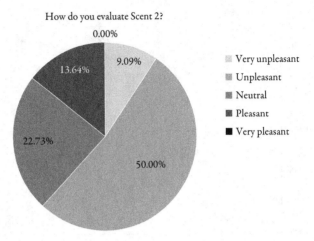

Figure 18. Response to the second question in laboratory conditions.

Table 11. Time course of excitement.

Second / Scent	1	2	3	4	5	6	7	8	9	10
Scent 1	**0.523**	0.506	0.493	0.501	0.479	0.468	0.466	0.454	0.460	0.453
Scent 2	0.535	0.532	0.528	0.527	0.537	0.558	0.550	0.596	**0.623**	0.567
Scent 3	0.682	**0.719**	**0.721**	**0.703**	**0.715**	**0.737**	**0.736**	**0.715**	0.693	0.676

The highest excitement score of 0.709 was evoked by scent 3 (Figure 19), which confirms that the strength of this emotion was relatively high in the respondents. On the one hand, the score of this scent is higher than the score of the other two for this emotion, but it is important to highlight that this score is also the highest achieved score compared to the other monitored emotions. In the case of engagement, we had higher values, but the highest score was only 0.598, which is a relatively lower value compared to 0.709. Based on these data, we can say that excitement was the strongest emotion experienced by respondents in this research. This may be explained be the fact that the respondents knew that they were going to smell some scents and, of course, they were trying to recognise them, which therefore influenced the expression of excitement.

Given its high score, we evaluate the effect of scent 3 positively. Based on the questionnaire results (Figure 20), we can also evaluate the effect of scent 3 positively. As many as 32% of respondents rated scent 3 as pleasant and 9% rated it as very pleasant. Scent 3 is the only one that respondents rated not only as pleasant, but also as very pleasant. On the other hand,

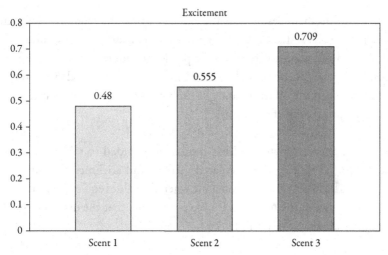

Figure 19. Score for excitement.

only 5% described this smell as very unpleasant and 36% as unpleasant, while 9% rated it as neutral. Based on this survey, the best rated smell was scent 3 (Herbs).

Using EEG and the Mind Your OSCs software, we also obtained long-term excitement values, and the results agree with the immediate excitement in that scent 3 had the most significant effect on a given emotion.

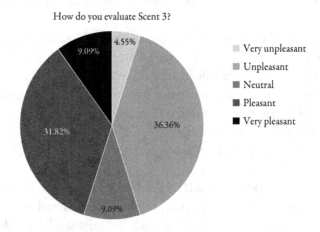

Figure 20. Response to the third question in laboratory conditions.

From the EEG measurement results, we also observed that the strength of the emotion changed (either increased or decreased) most often in the third or fourth second, for almost every emotion, so the effect of an aroma on the particular emotion was first demonstrated after 3-4 seconds, which is due to the delay of the EEG device and the delay that results from the connection between the olfactory and the limbic part of the brain that is responsible for controlling the processing of emotions.

When drawing conclusions from the EEG results, we decided to take into account the median values, too (Table 12). The calculated median and arithmetic mean values have minimal differences between them or even none when the values equal. Given that there are no big differences between the mean values, we can assume that the distribution of values in the file would be almost symmetrical.

The scent to be dispersed within the restaurant should evoke a high level of engagement and excitement and a low level of frustration and meditation (stress) in the consumers. The scent that met the most of the above criteria was scent 3. We monitored the highest level of engagement and excitement for it, while the lowest level of frustration was caused by scent 1 and the lowest level of stress by scent 2, but scent 3 was the second in both emotions.

During the testing of scents, in addition to EEG measurements, we also monitored the galvanic skin response using a mobile Shimmer3 GSR+. This device can provide us with valuable insights into the state of emotional excitement of the participant due to various stimuli, including smell. In general, GSR is a complementary method of monitoring for research carried out using EEG, eye tracker or for the analysis of facial expressions, or other methods.

GSR was monitored for the same time as the brain activity, i.e. 10 seconds. Based on the course for all three scents and on the average data of male respondents (Figure 21), we can conclude that the highest fluctuations (peaks) were mainly in the case of scents 1 and 2, thus their aromatic compounds acted as disturbing factors which caused galvanic resistance of the skin. In the case of scent 3, we monitored only 1 more pronounced peak, which was lower than those we see, for example, in scent 1. Also, the total course of galvanic resistance at scent 3 was below the level of 800 kOhm.

We saw similar results in female respondents, too (Figure 22). The most pronounced peaks were at scent 1, while there was only one more pronounced peak at scent 2 and in the case of scent 3 the fluctuations were very weak. It should also be noted that in the case of scents 2 and 3, the galvanic response was below the level of 1,300 kOhm. Based on GSR, we could evaluate scent 3 as the most positive one for all respondents (both gender groups), because its overall course was relatively constant, without recurrence of significant peaks and below

Table 12. Calculated median values for emotions.

Engagement

Second / Scent	1	2	3	4	5	6	7	8	9	10
Scent 1	0.552	0.552	0.552	0.552	0.552	0.552	0.552	0.552	0.552	0.552
Scent 2	0.552	0.552	0.552	0.552	0.552	0.552	0.552	0.552	0.552	0.552
Scent 3	0.552	0.552	0.552	0.552	0.552	0.552	0.552	0.552	0.552	0.552

Frustration

Second / Scent	1	2	3	4	5	6	7	8	9	10
Scent 1	0.426	0.432	0.422	0.422	0.425	0.425	0.421	0.417	0.415	0.409
Scent 2	0.463	0.462	0.459	0.458	0.457	0.463	0.464	0.468	0.471	0.468
Scent 3	0.438	0.441	0.445	0.449	0.450	0.452	0.453	0.456	0.473	0.473

Meditation

Second / Scent	1	2	3	4	5	6	7	8	9	10
Scent 1	0.333	0.333	0.333	0.333	0.333	0.333	0.333	0.333	0.333	0.333
Scent 2	0.333	0.333	0.333	0.333	0.333	0.333	0.333	0.333	0.333	0.333
Scent 3	0.333	0.333	0.333	0.333	0.333	0.333	0.333	0.333	0.333	0.333

Excitement

Second / Scent	1	2	3	4	5	6	7	8	9	10
Scent 1	0.491	0.420	0.478	0.498	0.461	0.450	0.445	0.414	0.402	0.428
Scent 2	0.546	0.463	0.545	0.503	0.505	0.536	0.483	0.614	0.628	0.573
Scent 3	0.697	0.718	0.749	0.797	0.821	0.818	0.792	0.784	0.623	0.569

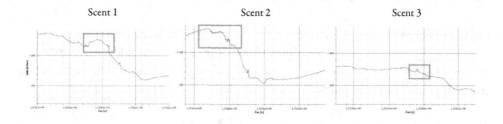

Figure 21. Outputs of GSR monitoring in male respondents.

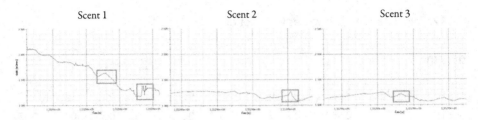

Figure 22. Outputs of GSR monitoring in female respondents.

the level of 800 kOhm and 1,300 kOhm, respectively. This smell had the least disturbing effect on test participants.

The laboratory research also included a questionnaire filled in during testing, and due to the nature of the data we obtained, we decided to use inductive statistics and specifically the Friedman test for analysing them (Appendix A). The reason for using this test was to find out if there is a statistically significant difference in the evaluation of scents – whether respondents rate all scents in the same way or they rate at least one pair of these scents differently.

The value of the calculated test statistic was 10.114 and the critical value was 5.991. Comparing these two values, we state that the test statistic is more extreme in the direction of the alternative than the critical value, which means we reject the null hypothesis in favour of the alternative hypothesis, i.e. the respondents evaluate at least one pair of these scents differently at a significance level of 0.05. We can therefore say that there is a statistically significant difference in the evaluation of scents.

The scent to be dispersed in the restaurant based on laboratory research results should influence both male and female customers, therefore we decided to find out if there is a statistically significant difference between male and female respondents in the evaluation of all three scents. For this purpose, we decided to use the Chi-Square Test of Independence to examine if there is no statistically significant difference between men and women in the evaluation of each scent or whether in fact there is (Appendix B).

In the case of scent 1, the calculated test statistic was 3.467, while the critical value was 7.815. By comparing these two values, we clearly see that the test statistic is less extreme than the critical value, and in this case we do not reject the null hypothesis, so there is no statistically significant difference between men and women in the evaluation of scent 1.

The calculated test statistic for scent 2 was 2.018, while the critical value was 7.815. Even in this case, the test statistic is less extreme than the critical value and we do not reject the null hypothesis, so there is no statistically significant difference between men and women in the evaluation of scent 2, too.

When evaluating scent 3, the calculated value of the test statistic was 5.833 and the critical value was 9.488, so even in this case our calculated test statistic is less extreme than the critical value. We do not reject the null hypothesis, so there is no statistically significant difference between men and women in the evaluation of scent 3.

In conclusion, we found that there is no statistically significant difference between men and women in the evaluation of the chosen 3 aromas.

During the research, we tried to ensure perfect laboratory conditions that would provide us with quality results. These and the participants' preferences are also influenced by their mood, so we asked about it in our survey, too. Bad mood demonstrates brain activity associated with decreased emotional resonance. The answers to this question (Figure 23) show that more than half of the respondents, namely 77.27% of them, were in a good mood during the laboratory testing process, and they stated they were feeling very well, comfortable or well.

After processing the results of laboratory research obtained using EEG and supplemented with GSR and a traditional questionnaire, we evaluated scent 3 (Herbs) as the one that had the best effect on the emotions of the participants. Testing of the effect of this scent then continued in the real conditions of the chosen restaurant.

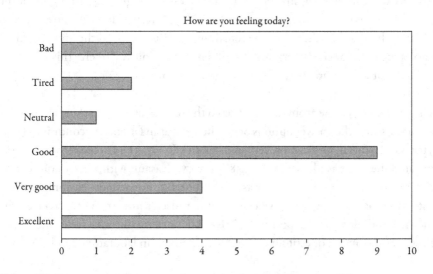

Figure 23. Response to the seventh question in laboratory conditions.

3.3 Testing under real conditions

We have supplemented our laboratory research with testing under real conditions, because testing in practice confirms and adds value as well as credibility to the achieved results.

The testing location consisted of the restaurant with an area of 72 m², for which we chose the professional aroma unit AromaStreamer 650 Bluetooth, which can be used for areas up to 150 m² (this device for aroma deployment in a restaurant was previously used in studies by *Berčík et al., 2020b, 2020c and Pavelka, 2019*). The aroma unit was set up as described in the methodology and placed in the restaurant.

Testing under real conditions consisted of monitoring the periods without and with aromatisation. The period without aromatisation lasted 2 weeks in March 2019, followed by a 2-week period with aromatisation in March and April the same year, where the number of sold pizza meals were chosen as the base for comparison. In addition, during the aromatisation period, we asked customers to complete a short questionnaire (Table 6) to find out whether they perceive the smell within the premises at all, how do they evaluate it as well as the age of participants, so the questionnaire contained 2 closed questions plus a demographic one. 57 customers (63.16% male and 36.84% female) agreed to fill in the questionnaire survey during the period under review (Table 7). Obtained primary data on the sale of meals and evaluation of the sales environment atmosphere were processed by descriptive statistics in the MATLAB software environment (*Cho and Martinez, 2014; Fisher and Marshall, 2009*).

Customers gave quite interesting answers to the first question (Figure 24) asking about the perception of aromatisation in the restaurant, since 68.42% responded with no awareness about a scent as the answer, while only the remaining 31.58% perceived the aromatisation. These answers suggest that customers probably did not consciously perceive this aroma, or rather considered it as a natural part of the restaurant or kitchen.

Customers who perceived the aroma also answered the second question, asking about their evaluation of the scent, the answer options being the same as in laboratory conditions (very pleasant, pleasant, neutral, unpleasant, very unpleasant). In Figure 25, we see that 42.11% of customers rated the scent as pleasant and 31.58% as very pleasant, with 21.05% considering it neutral, while 5.26% customers rated it as unpleasant, but not a single customer as very unpleasant. Based on these answers, we can say that those customers who perceived the aroma, evaluated the selected scent positively. This evaluation is in line with the one obtained by the selected aroma in the questionnaire survey carried out in laboratory conditions.

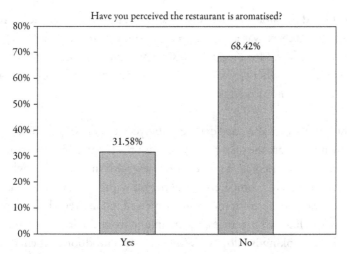

Figure 24. Response to the first question under real conditions.

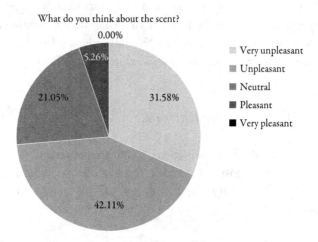

Figure 25. Response to the second question under real conditions.

As mentioned above, we compared the time periods by the number of pizza meals sold (Table 13). During both periods, it shows that Fridays, Saturdays and Sundays were popular days, because the place is visited by more people towards the end of the week (over 100 pizza meals were sold on Friday and Saturday, while the number during the week did not exceed 25).

We have also calculated the index of change for each day and we see that the biggest change was on Mondays, where there was a 30% decrease and on the other hand, a 29% increase was evidenced on Saturdays. However, the most important is the index of change for the entire period under review, where its value 1.12 means that the number of sold pizza meals increased by 12% over the monitored period.

In addition to these results, we also consider the employees' evaluation of aromatisation to be essential, since usually they are the ones perceiving it for the longest period of time. After the aromatisation period, we carried out a guided interview with the waitresses, who in general evaluated the scent positively. Compared to the period without aromatisation, during the aromatisation the area had one constant aroma dispersed, no matter what was prepared in the kitchen. The room has two entrances, the main one from the street and one that leads to the terrace, where smoking is allowed. When this second door is opened frequently, the unpleasant smell of cigarettes oozes to the restaurant. The waitresses highlighted that during the aromatisation, there was no unpleasant smell of cigarettes at all, despite the fact that the door was opened just as often. This statement is the result of the selected aroma containing a neutralising component, which has the ability to neutralise unpleasant odours (such as cigarettes or burned food) at the molecular level and is one of the most appreciated advantages of aroma marketing (*Air-Scent, 2017; Berčík, 2017*).

Table 13. Number of sold pizza meals.

Week / Day	Without aromatisation		With aromatisation		Index of change / day	Change / day in %
	13.03.2019 - 19.03.2019	20.03.2019 - 26.03.2019	27.03.2019 - 02.04.2019	03.04.2019 - 09.04.2019		
Monday	18	12	14	7	0.70	-30%
Tuesday	15	10	17	15	1.28	28%
Wednesday	21	19	15	21	0.90	-10%
Thursday	22	22	24	19	0.98	-2%
Friday	87	113	107	109	1.08	8%
Saturday	64	97	116	91	1.29	29%
Sunday	33	44	37	53	1.17	17%
TOTAL	260	317	330	315		
Index of change in the monitored period					1.12	
Change in the monitored period					12%	

As for the number of visitors to the restaurant, there was an increase in the second week of aromatisation. As this was mainly at lunch time, however, we cannot explicitly attribute it to the area being aromatised, as the nearby Indians Pub, which regularly offered a lunch menu, closed during the period, so the increase in lunchtime traffic may have been due to this fact.

We monitored another interesting result with the ordered types of pizza. The owner claims that the most ordered pizza types are Pizza Romantik and Pizza Quattro Formaggi (Four Cheese), but during the aromatised period, customers also started to order Pizza Venezia, which is herbal spicy, similar to the aroma that was dispersed. Until then, customers were not used to order this pizza, so the owner had been thinking about removing it from the menu for a long time. Despite the fact that 68.42% of customers stated that they do not perceive the aroma of the premises, we assume that the increase in demand for the mentioned pizza type may have been due to the impact of the selected scent on an unconscious level. As explained in the introduction and background, smells have an effect on an unconscious level and can influence the purchasing and consumer behaviour of customers, which we assume occurred in the observed period with aromatisation.

Overall, testing under real conditions brought quite essential and beneficial findings. The percentage increase in the number of pizza meals sold is not very high, but it should be taken into account that the aromatisation of the premises lasted only two weeks and still a certain rise was recorded. Assuming that the aromatisation would last longer, the increase would have probably been even higher.

Given that the restaurant has continuously rising sales, even a small percentage change would represent a high monetary value, from which, after quantifying the profit, it would be possible to purchase the aromatisation unit for approximately 900 EUR and refills for about 40 EUR. The aroma unit can also be rented, in which case the costs are approximately 100 EUR per month.

It is therefore recommended to aromatise the premises due to the positive evaluation experienced, both by employees who confirmed the neutralising effect of the selected scent, and by customers who evaluated the selected aroma positively. We do not consider the fact that some customers did not consciously perceive the aromatisation a negative result, because in conclusion, the aromatisation has an impact mainly on an unconscious level and it is rather likely that the increased demand for Pizza Venezia was due to the selected smell.

Chapter 4. Conclusion

It is without doubt that aromatisation affects consumer emotions, and today new technologies provide the option not only to effectively disperse these aromas, but especially to investigate their effect on consumer emotions. In addition to traditional research methods, consumer neuroscience tools come to the fore that allow us to obtain more in-depth and accurate information.

Consumer neuroscience offers various tools, including biometric or neuroimaging ones, and we decided to use one of these tools in this research – we chose electroencephalography (EEG) as a tool for monitoring the impact of aromas on consumer emotions. Prior to conducting research using EEG, thorough preparation was carried out, both in terms of gathering sufficient theoretical background as well as similar methodological procedures, studies and examples.

The research results might provide valuable information that could be used not only in the academic field, but also in practice, thus we were conducting the research in cooperation with the restaurant owner. In this case, the restaurant has been on the market for 20 years and has its loyal customers, but the owner is aware that there is always room to improve the customer experience and acquire new customers. She was already aware of the fact that aromatisation of premises can be used to enhance customer satisfaction, but since she did not know about specific examples of good practice in Slovakia, she agreed to provide information about her restaurant, as well as its premises as a location to carry out testing under real conditions.

The type of the restaurant and the GroupSolver results guided us in the selection of aromas. The chosen restaurant is mainly focused on selling pizza, so the selected aromas were to evoke an appetite in consumers, specifically a taste for pizza, which would then be reflected in sales and should also positively link consumers with the restaurant on an emotional level.

From the gastro aromas segment offered by Aroma Marketing, Ltd. we chose 3 scents that would complete the environment of the restaurant. The first scent, Pizza Salami, was the scent of pizza, the second was Whitebread, with the scent of white bread, and the third, Herbs, was an aromatic blend of herbs and spices. These 3 scents were tested by 22 participants of different age categories and economic status as part of a laboratory research.

The testing itself took place in an aromatisation box, which ensured controlled air conditions. We monitored the effect of the chosen 3 scents using an Emotiv mobile EEG device. We supplemented this neuroimaging method with a biometric method, by monitoring the galvanic skin response. Both methods belong to innovative research methods, but we also used the traditional method of information collecting, namely a questionnaire survey.

After processing the results and evaluating the effect of each aroma, we could conclude that scent 3 (Herbs) achieved the best results in terms of the impact on respondents' emotions. We have been observing emotions such as engagement, frustration, meditation and excitement. For each emotion, we monitored the course of a 10-second interval after smelling using an EEG device that recorded the values of each emotion, and the higher the recorded value was, the stronger the presence of the emotion in the respondent.

Electroencephalography recorded the highest scores for the emotions Engagement and Excitement, after smelling scent 3. The effect of this particular scent caused relatively higher values in the two emotions than the effect of scents 1 and 2, throughout the entire monitored period. Based on the results of the questionnaire survey from laboratory testing as well as from testing under real conditions, we can state that this scent had a positive effect, because it led most respondents to evaluate it positively, either as pleasant or very pleasant. The results of monitoring the galvanic skin response support the EEG results, because using this biometric method, we found that the composition of scent 3 had the least disturbing effect on respondents.

In addition to the two emotions mentioned, we have also been observing Frustration and Meditation. Frustration is more of a negative emotion that we do not want to evoke in consumers or customers of a restaurant, so its expression should not be strong. The lowest values of this emotion were recorded after smelling scent 1, followed by scent 3 and the highest level of frustration was caused by scent 2. Although the EEG results indicated that scent 1 caused the lowest level of frustration, based on the questionnaire survey, this smell was rated the most negative (27% of respondents rated it as very unpleasant and 45% as unpleasant). We assume that the strong presence of this emotion in the respondent is one of the factors leading to a negative rating, meaning that scent 1 that caused the lowest level of frustration should have a more positive rating than the other two scents, but this was not the case. By comparing these results, we see a certain discrepancy in conscious and unconscious evaluation.

In the case of Meditation, the lowest values were measured, which indicates that the scents caused a relatively weak subconscious effect, but based on the monitored values, the most positively evaluated scent was the one for which we recorded the highest values, i.e. scent 2, followed by scent 3 and then scent 1. Based on the questionnaire survey, half of the respondents rated scent 2 as unpleasant. It means that most probably a low level of negative subconscious influence is enough to lead the respondents to a negative evaluation of a smell.

We also supported the evaluation of each scent with inductive statistics. The Friedman test confirmed that there is statistically significant difference in the evaluation of scents and using the Chi-Square Test of Independence, we found that there is no statistically significant difference between men and women in their evaluation (both tests at the significance level of 0.05). This verification was necessary because the chosen restaurant is visited by both male and female customers and the selected aroma for aromatisation should be evaluated relatively equally by all customers. The purpose of aromatisation was to enhance the customer experience and to increase the appetite of all customers.

The results of research under laboratory conditions allowed us to choose scent 3 – Herbs to be deployed, which we subsequently tested under real conditions of the restaurant. This took place for 4 weeks and consisted of a period without aromatisation (two weeks) followed by a period with aromatisation (two weeks). During both periods, we monitored the number of pizza meals sold, which increased by 12% when comparing both periods.

In addition, the restaurant staff confirmed the effectiveness of the selected scent in neutralising unpleasant odours, such as cigarettes, which used to be smelt from the terrace into the restaurant. During aromatisation, customers were asked to fill out a short questionnaire, with the aim to find out whether they perceive the aromatisation at a conscious level and how they evaluate the selected scent. The survey results pointed to the fact that more than half of the customers who completed the questionnaire did not perceive the aromatisation at a conscious level. But on the other hand, the demand for the herbal-spicy Pizza Venezia (which smells similarly like the chosen aroma) has increased. Interestingly, the restaurant owner had been considering eliminating this pizza from the menu for a long time, because customers did not order it. It is very likely that the demand for this pizza was caused by the Herbs scent, thus demonstrating the effect of the selected scent on the unconscious level.

After evaluating the percentage increase for the observed period and the other benefits, it is highly recommended to consider continuing the aromatisation in the restaurant. After two weeks of aromatisation, there was a 12% increase in sales, and we assume that if the aromatisation lasted longer, the increase would probably be even higher. In addition, given the relatively high revenues of the restaurant, the purchase of an aromatisation unit of approximately 900 EUR, as well as refills of approximately 40 EUR or the rental of an aromatisation unit of approximately 100 EUR per month, it presents a profitable long-term investment. Except the financial point of view, the added value of aromatisation is the neutralisation of odours and positive evaluation by employees, as well as customer satisfaction and loyalty.

The research carried out in laboratory conditions was relatively complex, because we used the EEG neuroimaging method, the galvanic skin response biometric method and a traditional questionnaire survey. The price for conducting such research on a sample of 22 respondents would in practice range between 4,000-5,000 EUR, depending on the segment of the target group, according to the research agency 2muse (*Chovancová, 2018*).

This research provided an implicit and explicit verification of the effect of selected aromas on consumer emotions, as well as verification of the effectiveness of the selected aroma in practice.

One of the main recommendations of the research is to repeat the testing under real conditions, but for a longer period of time, for example 2 months or even longer.

Based on the owner's observations, one factor that causes the difference in the number of pizza meals sold during a certain month is whether it is before or after people receive their salary. Usually, after the payout period, the number of pizza meals sold is higher, so a recommendation would be to monitor this factor in the future, too.

In addition to conducting the present research and processing its results, there are other factors that could be changed in the future to ensure more accurate results and reciprocate them. Testing of selected aromas in laboratory conditions should take place at different moments of the day and at the same time at the beginning, in the middle and at the end of the week, because respondents' moods change both during the day and during the week.

Respondents' mood also changes due to the weather, so it is another factor that can skew the results. The solution in this case would be to perform aroma testing during rainy as well as sunny weather.

In a more detailed research, gas chromatography could be used, which would enable monitoring the air quality in the restaurant, because the air there is exposed to many more factors than that in the laboratory and at the same time other aromas could be tested under real conditions, too.

Another benefit of this research is the creation of a methodological procedure for monitoring the impact of aromas on consumer emotions, as well as education and dissemination of awareness of new research opportunities, using the tools of consumer neuroscience. Entrepreneurs often lack information about new opportunities that are available and effective, therefore this study provides beneficial information in this area.

References

Abe, T., 2005. Odor, Information and New Cosmetics – The Ripple Effect on Life by Aromachology Research. *Chemical Senses, 30*(1): i246-i247. https://doi.org/10.1093/chemse/bjh207

Abler, B., Walter, H. and Erk, S., 2005. Neural correlates of frustration. *Neuroreport, 16*(7): 669-672. https://doi.org/10.1097/00001756-200505120-00003

Achrol, R.S. and Kotler, P., 2012. Frontiers of the marketing paradigm in the third millennium. *Journal of the Academy of Marketing Science, 40*(1): 35-52. https://doi.org/10.1007/s11747-011-0255-4

AES (American Electroencephalographic Society)., 1994. Guideline Thirteen: Guidelines for Standard Electrode Position Nomenclature. *Journal Clinical Neurophysiology, 11*(1): 111-113.

Ahlert, D., Kenning, P. and Plassmann, H., 2006. A window to the consumer's mind: application of functional brain imaging techniques to advertising research. In: Diehl, S. and Terlutter, R. (eds) *International Advertising and Communication*. Springer, GWV Fachverlage, Wiesbaden, Germany, pp. 163-178. https://doi.org/10.1007/3-8350-5702-2_9

Air-Scent International, 2017. *Scent Marketing: 11 Research-Backed Benefits To Bottom Line.* Available at: https://www.airscent.com/scent-marketing-11-research-backed-benefits-to-bottom-line-profits/

Alpha Aromatics, 2018. *The Aromatic Sources & Fragrant Compounds Used In Perfumery.* Available at: https://www.alphaaromatics.com/blog/aromatic-sources-fragrant-compounds-in-perfumery/

Alwitt, L.F., 1985. EEF Activity Reflects the Content of Commercials. *Psychol. Process. Advert. Eff. Theory Res. Appl. 1985, 13*: 209-219.

Ariely, D. and Berns, G.S., 2010. Neuromarketing: The hope and hype of neuroimaging in business. *Nature Reviews Neuroscience, 11*(4): 284-292. https://doi.org/10.1038%2Fnrn2795

Aroma Marketing, 2017. *Dokáže vôňa čokolády zvýšiť predaj kníh?* Available at: https://www.aromarketing.sk/dokaze-vona-cokolady-zvysit-predaj-knih

Aroma Marketing, 2020. *Segmenty vôní.* Available at: https://www.aromarketing.sk/segmenty-voni

Aroma Marketing, 2021. *Aroma Streamer 650 Bluetooth.* Available at: https://www.aromarketing.sk/aroma-streamer-650-bluetooth

Aromatech, 2017. *The Benefits Of Scenting In The 21st Century.* Available at: https://aromatechscent.com/blogs/home-scenting-essentials-blog/the-benefits-of-scenting-in-the-21st-century

Aromatech, 2018. *What's In An Aroma? Scent Therapy Explained.* Available at: https://aromatechscent.com/blogs/home-scenting-essentials-blog/what-s-in-an-aroma-scent-therapy-explained

Badcock, N.A., Mousikou, P., Mahajan, Y., de Lissa, P., Thie, J. and McArthur, G., 2013. Validation of the Emotiv EPOC® EEG gaming system for measuring research quality auditory ERPs. *PeerJ, 1*: e38. https://doi.org/10.7717/peerj.38

Bartholmé, R.H. and Melewar T.C., (2011). Remodelling the Corporate Visual Identity Construct: A Reference to the Sensory and Auditory Dimension. *Corporate Communications: An International Journal, 16*(1): 53-64. https://doi.org/10.1108/13563281111100971

Batt, R., 2018. *KHJ Brand Activation – Ah, The Sweet Smell of Brand Success.* Available at: https://www.khj.com/scent-marketing/

Bell, S., 2006. Future sense: defining brands through scent. *GDR Creative Intelligence, 21*: 1-5. https://api.natscent. com/pdf/5_bell_and_bell_futuresense.pdf

Bercea, M.D., 2013. Quantitative versus Qualitative in Neuromarketing Research. In *Munich Personal RePEc Archive*. MPRA Paper No. 44134, Munich University Library, Munich, Germany. Available at: https://mpra.ub.uni-muenchen.de/id/eprint/44134

Berčík, J., 2017. Jakub Berčík: Je aromatizácia predajní a tvorba čuchovej značky zárukou úspechu? In: *Tovar a Predaj*. ISSN 1805-0549. Available at: https://www.tovarapredaj.sk/2017/12/13/jakub-bercik-je-aromatisacia-predajni-a-tvorba-cuchovej-znacky-zarukou-uspechu/

Berčík, J., 2018. Jakub Berčík: Ktorá vianočná vôňa vás dostane? In: Tovar a Predaj. ISSN 1805-0549. Available at: https://www.tovarapredaj.sk/2018/12/20/ktora-vianocna-vona-vas-dostane/

Berčík, J. and Horská, E., 2015. Sound System and Noise as Essential Elements of Visual Merchandising in Selected Retail Chains in the Slovak Republic. European Journal of Business Science and Technology, 1(1): 15-23. Available at: https://www.ejobsat.cz/wp-content/uploads/2015/10/EJOBSAT150101_001.pdf

Berčík, J., Gálová, J., Neomániová, K., Mravcová, A., Vietoris, V., 2020a. Metodika skúmania vplyvu aromatizácie v obchode a službách s využitím inovatívnych nástrojov na získavanie spätnej väzby. SPU, Nitra, Slovak Republic, 71 pp. ISBN 978-80-552-2294-3.

Berčík, J., Mravcová, A., Gálová, J. and Mikláš, M., 2020b. The use of consumer neuroscience in aroma marketing of a service company. Potravinarstvo Slovak Journal of Food Sciences, 14(1/2020): 1200-1210. https://doi.org/10.5219/1465

Berčík, J., Neomániová, K., Gálová, J. and Mravcová, A., 2021a. Consumer Neuroscience as a Tool to Monitor the Impact of Aromas on Consumer Emotions When Buying Food. Applied Sciences, 11(15): 6692, pp. 1-17. https://doi.org/10.3390/app11156692

Berčík, J., Neomániová, K., Mravcová, A. and Gálová, J., 2021b. Review of the Potential of Consumer Neuroscience for Aroma Marketing and Its Importance in Various Segments of Services. Applied Sciences, 11(16): 7636. https://doi.org/10.3390/app11167636

Berčík, J., Paluchová, J., Gálová, J., Neomániová, K. 2019. Metodika skúmania vplyvu aromatizácie s využitím nástrojov spotrebiteľskej neurovedy vo výrobe, obchode a službách. SPU, Nitra, Slovak Republic, 43 pp. ISBN 978-80-552-2127-4.

Berčík, J., Paluchová, J., Vietoris, V. and Horská, E., 2016. Placing of Aroma Compounds by Food Sales Promotion in Chosen Services Business. Potravinarstvo Slovak Journal of Food Sciences, 10(1): 672-679. ISSN 1337-0960. https://doi.org/10.5219/666

Berčík, J., Virágh, R., Kádeková, Z. and Duchoňová, T., 2020c. Aroma marketing as a tool to increase turnover in a chosen business entity. Potravinarstvo Slovak Journal of Food Sciences, 14(1/2020): 1161-1175. https://doi.org/10.5219/1475

Bergland, C., 2015. How Does Scent Drive Human Behavior? Psychology Today. ISSN 0033-3107. Available at: https://www.psychologytoday.com/us/blog/the-athletes-way/201506/how-does-scent-drive-human-behavior

Berka, C., Levendowski, D.J., Lumicao, M.N., Yau, A., Davis, G., Zivkovic, V.T., Olmstead, R.E., Tremoulet, P.D. and Craven, P.L., 2007. EEG correlates of task engagement and mental workload in vigilance, learning, and memory tasks. Aviation, Space, and Environmental Medicine, 78(5 Suppl): B231-B244.

Biswas, D., Labrecque, L. I., Lehmann, D. R. and Markos, E., 2014. Making Choices While Smelling, Tasting, and Listening: The Role of Sensory (Dis)similarity When Sequentially Sampling Products. Journal of Marketing, 78(1): 112-126. https://doi.org/10.1509/jm.12.0325

Boesveldt, S. and de Graaf, K., 2017. The Differential Role of Smell and Taste for Eating Behavior. Perception, 46(3-4): 307-319. https://doi.org/10.1177%2F0301006616685576

Bone, P.F. and Jantrania, S., 1992. Olfaction as a cue for product quality. Marketing Letters, 3: 289-296. https://doi.org/10.1007/BF00994136

Bosmans, A., 2006. Scents and Sensibility: When Do (In)Congruent Ambient Scents Influence Product Evaluations? Journal of Marketing, 70(3, July 2006): 32-43. https://www.jstor.org/stable/30162099

Bowen, J., 2016. Can smell and scents really affect workplace productivity? Initial. Available at: https://www.initial.co.uk/blog/can-smell-really-affect-workplace-productivity/

Bradford, D.K. and Desrochers, M.D., 2009. The Use of Scents to Influence Consumers: The Sense of Using Scents to Make Cents. Journal of Business Ethics, 90(2): 141-153. ISSN 1573-0697. https://doi.org/10.1007/s10551-010-0377-5

Brann, J.H. and Firestein, S.J., 2014. A lifetime of neurogenesis in the olfactory system. Frontiers in Neuroscience, 8(182): 1-11. https://doi.org/10.3389/fnins.2014.00182

Brumfield, C. R., Goldney, J. and Gunning, S., 2008. Whiff! The Revolution of Scent Communications in the Information Age. Quimby Press, New York, 334 pp.

Calvert, G.A., and Brammer, M.J., 2012. Predicting Consumer Behavior: Using Novel Mind-Reading Approaches. IEEE Pulse 3(3, May 2012): 38-41. https://doi.org/10.1109/MPUL.2012.2189167

Calvert, G., Spence, C. and Stein, B.E., 2004. Handbook of Multisensory Processes. MIT Press, Cambridge, MA, USA, 950 pp.

Calvo-Porral, C., Ruiz-Vega, A. and Lévy-Mangin, J.-P., 2019. The Influence of Consumer Involvement in Wine Consumption-Elicited Emotions. Journal of International Food & Agribusiness Marketing, 31(2): 128-149. https://doi.org/10.1080/08974438.2018.1482587

Čarnogurský, K., Diačiková, A. and Madzík, P., 2021. The Impact of the Aromatization of Production Environment on Workers: A Systematic Literature Review. Applied Sciences, 11(12): 5600. https://doi.org/10.3390/app11125600

Cherubino, P., Martinez-Levy, A. C., Caratù, M., Cartocci, G., Di Flumeri, G., Modica, E., Rossi, D., Mancini, M. and Trettel, A., 2019. Consumer Behaviour through the Eyes of Neurophysiological Measures: State-of-the-Art and Future Trends. Computational Intelligence and Neuroscience, 2019: 1976847. https://doi.org/10.1155/2019/1976847

Cho, M. and Martinez, W.L., 2015. Statistics in MATLAB: A Primer. Chapman and Hall/CRC.

Chovancová, L., 2018, November 21. Vianočné pozdravy 2018. Prvý čuchový test vianočných vôní. EEG meranie v kombinácii s facereaderom: záverečná správa [Paper presentation]. Agentúra 2muse, Bratislava.

Ciorciari, J., 2012. Bioelectrical signals: The electroencephalogram. In: Wood, A. (ed.) Physiology, Biophysics and Biomedical Engineering. Taylor & Francis, pp. 539-566. https://doi.org/10.1201/b11558

Clark, P., 2009. Running Head: Management overview of Scent as a Marketing Communications Tool: SMC Working Paper. Zug: SMC University. 20 pp. Available at: https://www.smcuniversity.com/working_papers/Paul_Clark_-_Running_Head_-_Management_overview_of_Scent_as_a_Marketing_Communications_Tool.pdf

Cleary, A.M., Konkel, K.E., Nomi, J.S. and McCabe, D.P., 2010. Odor Recognition Without Identification. Memory & Cognition, 38(4): 452-460. https://doi.org/10.3758/MC.38.4.452

Coelli, S., Sclocco, R., Barbieri, R., Reni, G., Zucca, C. and Bianchi, A.M., 2015. EEG-based index for engagement level monitoring during sustained attention. 37th Annual International Conference of the IEEE Engineering in Medicine and Biology Society (EMBC), pp. 1512-1515. IEEE. https://doi.org/10.1109/EMBC.2015.7318658

Costa, M.F., Patricia, Z., Natasha, R., Jessica, A. and Maria, G.V., 2012. Sensory marketing: consumption experience of the Brazilian in the restaurant industry. International Journal of Business Strategy, 12(4): 165-171.

Deveney, C.M., Connolly, M.E., Haring, C.T., Bones, B.L., Reynolds, R.C., Kim, P., Pine, D.S. and Leibenluft, E., 2013. Neural mechanisms of frustration in chronically irritable children. The American Journal of Psychiatry, 170(10): 1186-1194. https://doi.org/10.1176/appi.ajp.2013.12070917

Doty, R.L. and Kamath, V., 2014. The influences of age on olfaction: a review. Frontiers in Psychology, 5(20): 1-20. https://doi.org/10.3389/fpsyg.2014.00020

Doucé, L. and Janssens, W., 2013. The Presence of a Pleasant Ambient Scent in a Fashion Store: The Moderating Role of Shopping Motivation and Affect Intensity. Environment and Behavior, 45(2): 215-238. https://doi.org/10.1177%2F0013916511410421

Duvinage, M., Castermans, T., Petieau, M., Hoellinger, T., Cheron, G. and Dutoit, T., 2013. Performance of the Emotiv EPOC headset for P300-based applications. BioMedical Engineering OnLine, 12(1): 56. Available at: http://www.biomedical-engineering-online.com/content/12/1/56

Ekebas, C., 2015. 'The Magic Formula: Scent and Brand' – The Influence of Olfactory Sensory Co-Branding on Consumer Evaluations and Experiences: dissertation. Old Dominion University, 120 pp. https://doi.org/10.25777/3w6j-3806 https://digitalcommons.odu.edu/businessadministration_etds/24

Emotiv, 2014. EMOTIV EPOC User Manual – Headset and software setup for your Emotiv EPOC neuroheadset. Available at: https://s3.amazonaws.com/emotiv-web/wp_document_public/EPOCUserManual2014.pdf

Emotiv, 2019. EPOC+ User Manual. Available at: https://emotiv.gitbook.io/epoc-user-manual/

Emotiv, 2020. EPOC+ User Manual – About. Available at: https://emotiv.gitbook.io/epoc-user-manual/introduction-1/about

Emsenhuber, B., 2011. Scent Marketing: Making Olfactory Advertising Pervasive. In: Müller, J., Alt, F. and Michelis, D. (eds) Pervasive Advertising. Human-Computer Interaction Series. Springer, London, UK, pp. 343-360. https://doi.org/10.1007/978-0-85729-352-7_17

ESOMAR, 2012. 36 Questions to Help Commission Neuroscience Research. Available at: https://www.esomar.org/uploads/public/knowledge-and-standards/codes-and-guidelines/ESOMAR_36-Questions-to-help-commission-neuroscience-research.pdf

Ezzatdoost, K., Hojjati, H. and Aghajan, H., 2020. Decoding olfactory stimuli in EEG data using nonlinear features: A pilot study. Journal of Neuroscience Methods, 341: 108870. https://doi.org/10.1016/j.jneumeth.2020.108780

Farnsworth, B., 2019. EEG (Electroencephalography): The Complete Pocket Guide. Available at: https://imotions.com/blog/eeg/

Feinberg, F.M., Kinnear, T. and Taylor, J.R., 2012. Modern Marketing Research: Concepts, Methods, and Cases. South-Western College Pub, 720 pp.

Firestein, S., 2001. How the olfactory system makes sense of scents. Nature, 413(6852): 211-218. https://doi.org/10.1038/35093026

Fisher, C. E., Chin, L. and Klitzman, R., 2010. Defining neuromarketing: Practices and professional challenges. Harvard Review of Psychiatry, 18(4): 230-237. https://doi.org/10.3109/10673229.2010.496623

Fisher, M.J. and Marshall, A.P., 2009. Understanding descriptive statistics. Australian Critical Care, 22(2): 93-97. https://doi.org/10.1016/j.aucc.2008.11.003

Franěk, M., 2007. Hudební psychologie. Karolinum, Praha, Czech Republic, 240 pp.

Giacalone, D., Pierański, B. and Borusiak, B., 2021. Aromachology and Customer Behavior in Retail Stores: A Systematic Review. Applied Sciences, 11(13): 6195. https://doi.org/10.3390/app11136195

Giraldo, S. and Ramirez, R., 2013. Brain-activity-driven real-time music emotive control. In Luck, G. & Brabant, O. (eds) Proceedings of the 3rd International Conference on Music & Emotion (ICME3), Jyväskylä, Finland, 11th-15th June 2013. http://mtg.upf.edu/node/2893

Girard, C., 2017. Meet the Scent Marketing Firm Winning the Battle for Your Nose. Available at: https://www.nbcnews.com/business/your-business/meet-scent-marketing-firm-winning-battle-your-nose-n783761

Girona-Ruíz, D., Cano-Lamadrid, M., Carbonell-Barrachina, Á.A., López-Lluch, D. and Sendra, E., 2021. Aromachology Related to Foods, Scientific Lines of Evidence: A Review. Applied Sciences, 11(13): 6095. https://doi.org/10.3390/app11136095

Glaenzer, E., 2016. Are the Brain and the Mind One? Neuromarketing and How Consumers Make Decisions: Honors Thesis. Colby College, Waterville, 53 pp. Available at: http://digitalcommons.colby.edu/honorstheses/812

Gómez Ramírez, C., Manzi Puertas, M.A. and Galindo Becerra, T., 2017. El scent marketing: una revisión bibliográfica. Pensamiento y Gestión, 37: 215-255. ISSN 1657-6276. https://doi.org/10.14482/pege.37.7027

GroupSolver, 2021a. GroupSolver – Product – How It Works. Available at: https://www.groupsolver.com/how-it-works/

GroupSolver, 2021b. GroupSolver – Resources – FAQ – Product. Available at: https://www.groupsolver.com/faqs/

Grybś-Kabocik, M., 2018. The scent marketing: consumers perception. The Business and Management Review, 9(4): 483-486. https://cberuk.com/cdn/conference_proceedings/2019-07-13-11-33-09-AM.pdf

Guéguen, N. and Petr, C., 2006. Odors and consumer behavior in a restaurant. International Journal of Hospitality Management, 25(2): 335-339. https://doi.org/10.1016/j.ijhm.2005.04.007

Haghighi, A. and Klein, D., 2010, July. An entity-level approach to information extraction. In Proceedings of the ACL 2010 Conference Short Papers. Association for Computational Linguistics, pp. 291-295.

Hairston, W.D., Whitaker, K.W., Ries, A.J., Vettel, J.M., Bradford, J.C., Kerick, S.E. and McDowell, K., 2014. Usability of four commercially-oriented EEG systems. Journal of Neural Engineering, 11(4): 046018. https://doi.org/10.1088/1741-2560/11/4/046018

Harris, D., 2017. Engineering Psychology and Cognitive Ergonomics: Cognition and Design. In: 14th International Conference on Engineering Psychology and Cognitive Ergonomics, EPCE 2017, Held as Part of HCI International 2017, Vancouver, BC, Canada, July 9-14, 2017, Proceedings, Part II. Springer International Publishing, New York, USA, 439 pp. ISBN 978-3-319-5847-4. https://doi.org/10.1007/978-3-319-58475-1

Harris, J.M., Ciorciari, J. and Gountas, J., 2018. Consumer neuroscience for marketing researchers. Journal of Consumer Behavior, 17(3): 239-252. https://doi.org/10.1002/cb.1710

Hassan, I. and Iqbal, J., 2016. Employing Sensory Marketing as a Promotional Advantage for Creating Brand Differentiation and Brand Loyalty. Pakistan Journal of Commerce and Social Sciences, 10(3): 725-734. ISSN 1997-8553. Available at http://www.jespk.net/publications/333.pdf

Hayes, J.E. and Keast, R.S.J., 2011. Two decades of supertasting: where do we stand? Physiology & Behavior, 104(5): 1072-1074. https://doi.org/10.1016%2Fj.physbeh.2011.08.003

HBR – Harvard Business Review, 2015. The Science of Sensory Marketing. Available at: https://hbr.org/2015/03/the-science-of-sensory-marketing

Helmenstine, A.M., 2019. Aroma Compounds and Their Odors. Available at: https://www.thoughtco.com/aroma-compounds-4142268

Hensel, D., Iorga, A., Wolter, L. and Znanewitz, J., 2017. Conducting neuromarketing studies ethically-practitioner perspectives. Cogent Psychology, 4: 1-13. https://doi.org/10.1080/23311908.2017.1320858

Herrmann, A., Zidansek, M., Sprott, D.E. and Spangenberg, E.R., 2013. The Power of Simplicity: Processing Fluency and the Effects of Olfactory Cues on Retail Sales. Journal of Retailing, 89(1): 30-43. https://doi.org/10.1016/j.jretai.2012.08.002

Herz, R.S. 2009. Aromatherapy Facts and Fictions: A Scientific Analysis of Olfactory Effects on Mood, Physiology and Behavior. International Journal of Neuroscience, 119(2): 263-290. https://doi.org/10.1080/00207450802333953

Herz, R.S., 2010. The emotional, cognitive, and biological basics of olfaction: Implications and considerations for scent marketing. In: Krishna, A. (ed.) Sensory Marketing: Research on the Sensuality of Products. Routledge. New York, NY, USA, pp. 87-107.

Ho, C. and Spence, C., 2005. Olfactory facilitation of dual-task performance. Neuroscience Letters, 389(1): 35-40. https://doi.org/10.1016/j.neulet.2005.07.003

Hultén, B., Broweus, N. and van Dijk, M., 2009. Sensory Marketing. Palgrave Macmillan, London, UK, 197 pp. https://doi.org/10.1057/9780230237049

Hurt, J., 2012. Looking To Learn: Why Visuals Are So Important. Available at: https://velvetchainsaw.com/2012/03/01/looking-learn-why-visuals-so-important/

Hussain, S., 2019. Sensory Marketing Strategies and Consumer Behavior: Sensible Selling Using All Five Senses. The IUP Journal of Business Strategy, 16(3/September 2019): 34-44. Available at: https://ssrn.com/abstract=3792792

Ilijima, M., Nio, E., Nashimoto, E. and Iwata, M., 2007. Effects of aroma on the autonomic nervous system and brain activity under stress conditions. Autonomic Neuroscience: Basic & Clinical, 135(1-2): 97-98. https://doi.org/10.1016/j.autneu.2007.06.161

iMotions, 2019. Electroencephalography – The Complete Pocket Guide. 59 pp. Available online on demand.

iMotions, 2020. Galvanic Skin Response The Complete Pocket Guide. Available at: https://imotions.com/gsr-guide-ebook/

Jackson, A., 2018. Can retailers increase sales through scent marketing? Premium Scenting Available at: https://www.premiumscenting.com/blog/retailers-increase-sales-scent-marketing/

Jiménez Marín, G. and Elías Zambrano, R., 2018. Marketing sensorial: merchandising a través de las emociones en el punto de venta. Análisis de un caso. adComunica. Revista Científica de Estrategias, Tendencias e Innovación en Comunicación, 15: 235-253. https://doi.org/10.6035/2174-0992.2018.15.12

Kádeková, Z., Košičiarová, I., Holotová, M., Kubicová, Ľ., Predanócyová, K., 2020. Aromachology and its role in influencing consumer behaviour of millennials. International Scientific Days 2020. Szent István University, Gödöllö Hungary, pp. 119-129. https://doi.org/10.18515/dBEM.ISD.P01.2020

Karr, D., 2020. Scent Marketing: Statistics, Olfactory Science, And The Industry. Available at: https://martech.zone/what-is-scent-marketing/

Kashyap, A.K., 2015. Revitalize Your Restaurant by Enhancing its Servicescape. International Journal of Engineering Technology, Management and Applied Sciences, 3(12): 12-23. http://www.ijetmas.com/admin/resources/project/paper/f201512131450001757.pdf

Kenning, P. and Plassmann, H., 2005. NeuroEconomics: an overview from an economic perspective. Brain Research Bulletin, 67(5): 343-354. https://doi.org/10.1016/j.brainresbull.2005.07.006

Kenning, P.H. and Plassmann, H., 2008. How neuroscience can inform consumer research. IEEE Transactions on Neural Systems and Rehabilitation Engineering, 16(6): 532-538. https://doi.org/10.1109/tnsre.2008.2009788

Khushaba, R.N., Wise, C., Kodagoda, S., Louviere, J., Kahn, B. E. and Townsend, C., 2013. Consumer neuroscience: Assessing the brain response to marketing stimuli using electroencephalogram (EEG) and eye tracking. Expert Systems with Applications, 40(9): 3803-3812. ISSN 0957-4174. https://doi.org/10.1016/j.eswa.2012.12.095

Kleinová, K. and Vilhanová, L., 2013. Marketing communications at the point of sale from the customer's point of view. In Wybrane aspekty zarządzania marketingowego. Wydawnictwo SGGW, Warsaw, Poland, pp. 75-87.

Konagai, C., Hamada, M., Nguyen, V.C. and Koga, Y., 2002. The effect of the aroma from soybeans after heating on EEG. International Congress Series, 1232: 119-123. https://doi.org/10.1016/S0531-5131(01)00725-7

Kotler, P., 2011. Marketing insights from A to Z: 80 concepts every manager needs to know. Wiley, Hoboken, NJ, USA, 224 pp.

Krbot Skorić, M., Adamec, I., Branka Jerbić, A., Gabelić, T., Hajnšek, S. and Habek, M., 2014. Electroencephalographic Response to Different Odors in Healthy Individuals: A Promising Tool for Objective Assessment of Olfactory Disorders. Clinical EEG and Neuroscience, 46(4): 370-376. https://doi.org/10.1177/1550059414545649

Krishna, A., 2012. An integrative review of sensory marketing: Engaging the senses to affect perception, judgment and behavior. Journal of Consumer Psychology, 22(3): 332-351. https://doi.org/10.1016/j.jcps.2011.08.003

Krishna, A., Cian, L. and Sokolova, T., 2016. The power of sensory marketing in advertising. Current Opinion in Psychology, 10(August 2016): 142-147. https://doi.org/10.1016/j.copsyc.2016.01.007

Krishna, A., Lwin, M.O. and Morrin, M., 2010. Product Scent and Memory. Journal of Consumer Research, 37(1): 57–67. https://doi.org/10.1086/649909

Krugman, H.E., 1971. Brain wave measures of media involvement. Journal of Advertising Research, 11(1): 3-9.

Kuczamer-Kłopotowska, S., 2017. Sensory marketing as a new tool of supporting the marketing communication process in tourism services sector. Handel Wewnętrzny, 2(367): 226-235. ISSN 0438-5403. Available at: http://cejsh.icm.edu.pl/cejsh/element/bwmeta1.element.desklight-b6a46dc2-5a96-4abf-979f-66267091489b/c/IBRKK-handel_wew_2-2017.226-235.pdf

Lange, C., Kuch, B. and Metzger, J.W., 2015. Occurrence and fate of synthetic musk fragrances in a small German river. Journal of Hazardous Materials, 282: 34-40. https://doi.org/10.1016/j.jhazmat.2014.06.027

Laros, F.J. and Steenkamp, J.B., 2005. Emotions in consumer behavior: A hierarchical approach. Journal of Business Research, 58(10): 1437-1445. https://doi.org/10.1016/j.jbusres.2003.09.013

Lawless, H.T. and Heymann, H., 2010. Sensory Evaluation of Food: Principles and Practices. Springer-Verlag New York, New York, USA, 596 pp.

Lehrner, J., Marwinski, G., Lehr, S., Johren, P. and Deecke, L., 2005. Ambient odors of orange and lavender reduce anxiety and improve mood in a dental office. Physiology & Behavior, 86(1-2): 92-95. https://doi.org/10.1016/j.physbeh.2005.06.031

Li, J., Streletskaya, N.A. and Gómez, M.I. 2019. Does taste sensitivity matter? The effect of coffee sensory tasting information and taste sensitivity on consumer preferences. Food Quality and Preference, 71: 447-451. https://doi.org/10.1016/j.foodqual.2018.08.006

Li, W., Moallem, I., Paller, K. A. and Gottfried, J.A., 2007. Subliminal Smells Can Guide Social Preferences. Psychological Science, 18(12): 1044-1049. https://doi.org/10.1111/j.1467-9280.2007.02023.x

Lin, M.H., Cross, S.N.N. and Childers, T.L., 2018a. Understanding olfaction and emotions and the moderating role of individual differences. European Journal of Marketing, 52(3/4): 811-836. https://doi.org/10.1108/EJM-05-2015-0284

Lin, M.H., Cross, S.N.N., Jones, W.J. and Childers, T.L., 2018b. Applying EEG in consumer neuroscience. European Journal of Marketing, 52(1/2): 66-91. https://doi.org/10.1108/EJM-12-2016-0805

Lu, Z.M., Xu, W., Yu, N.H., Zhou, T., Li, G.Q., Shi, J.S. and Xu, Z.H., 2011. Recovery of aroma compounds from Zhenjiang aromatic vinegar by supercritical fluid extraction. International Journal of Food Science & Technology, 46(7): 1508-1514. https://doi.org/10.1111/j.1365-2621.2011.02649.x

Madzharov, A.V., Block, L.G. and Morrin, M., 2015. The Cool Scent of Power: Effects of Ambient Scent on Consumer Preferences and Choice Behavior. Journal of Marketing, 79(1): 83-96. https://doi.org/10.1509/jm.13.0263

Martin, K.D. and Smith, N.C., 2008. Commercializing Social Interaction: The Ethics of Stealth Marketing. Journal of Public Policy & Marketing, 27(1): 45-56. https://doi.org/10.1509/jppm.27.1.45

Mattila, A.S. and Wirtz, J., 2001. Congruency of scent and music as a driver of in-store evaluations and behavior. Journal of Retailing, 77(2): 273-289. https://doi.org/10.1016/S0022-4359(01)00042-2

McMahan, T., Parberry, I. and Parsons, T.D., 2015. Evaluating Player Task Engagement and Arousal Using Electroencephalography. Procedia Manufacturing, 3(2015): 2303-2310. https://doi.org/10.1016/j.promfg.2015.07.376

Minsky, L., Fahey, C. and Fabrigas, C., 2018, April 11. Inside the Invisible but Influential World of Scent Branding. Harvard Business Review. Available at: https://hbr.org/2018/04/inside-the-invisible-but-influential-world-of-scent-branding.

Mobley, A.S., Rodriguez-Gil, D.J., Imamura, F. and Greer, C.A., 2014. Aging in the olfactory system. Trends in neurosciences, 37(2): 77-84. https://doi.org/10.1016/j.tins.2013.11.004

Morrin, M. and Ratneshwar, S., 2003. Does It Make Sense to Use Scents to Enhance Brand Memory? Journal of Marketing Research, 40(1): 10-25. https://doi.org/10.1509/jmkr.40.1.10.19128

Moss, M., Hewitt, S., Moss, L. and Wesnes, K., 2008. Modulation of cognitive performance and mood by aromas of peppermint and ylang-ylang. The International Journal of Neuroscience, 118(1): 59-77. https://doi.org/10.1080/00207450601042094

Moya, I., García-Madariaga, J. and Blasco, M.-F., 2020. What Can Neuromarketing Tell Us about Food Packaging? Foods, 9(12): 1856. https://doi.org/10.3390/foods9121856

Mravcová, A., 2019. Environmental awareness and environmental citizenship dimension. Slovak Journal of Political Sciences, 19(2): 32-48. ISSN 1338-3140.

Mušinská, K., Horská, E., Paluchová, J., Beňovičová, K., 2020. Aroma Marketing and Its Impact on the Sales Success and the Economic Situation in Café InCuple. In: Challenges and changes under the shadow of COVID-19. Szent István University, Gödöllö, Hungary, pp. 202-212. ISBN 978-963-269-930-1.

Nadányiová, M., 2017. Zmyslový marketing ako nástroj budovania značky na medzinárodnom trhu – Sensory Marketing as a Tool of Brand Building in the International Market. Medzinárodné Vzťahy – Journal of International Relations, 15(4): 371-389. ISSN 1339-2751. Available at: https://econpapers.repec.org/scripts/redir.pf?u=http%3A%2F%2Ffmv.euba.sk%2FRePEc%2Fbrv%2Fjournl%2FMV2017-4.pdf;h=repec:brv:journl:v:15:y:2017:i:4:p:371-389

Nagyová, Ľ., Berčík, J., Džupina, M., Hazuchová, N., Holienčinová, M., Kádeková, Z., Koprda, T., Košičiarová, I., Récky, R. and Rybanská, J., 2018. Marketing II. SPU v Nitre, Nitra, Slovak Republic, 453 pp. ISBN 978-80-552-1943-1.

Newson, J., 2017. What does EEG have to do with Perfume? Available at: https://sapienlabs.co/eeg-and-perfume/

Nghiêm-Phú, B., 2017. Sensory marketing in an outdoor out-store shopping environment – an exploratory study in Japan. Asia Pacific Journal of Marketing and Logistics, 29(5): 994-1016. https://doi.org/10.1108/APJML-09-2016-0178

Nibbe, N. and Orth, R.U., 2017. Odor in Marketing. In: Buettner, A. (ed.) Springer Handbook of Odor. Springer Handbooks, Springer, Cham, Switzerland, pp. 141-142. https://doi.org/10.1007/978-3-319-26932-0_56

Nielsen, 2015. I Second That Emotion: The Emotive Power Of Music In Advertising. Available at: http://www.nielsen.com/us/en/insights/news/2015/i-second-that-emotion-the-emotivepower-of-music-in-advertising.html

NMSBA – Neuromarketing Science & Business Association, 2020. Neuromarketing Yearbook 2020 – Best Practices, Research and an overview of the year. Neuromarketing Science & Business Association, AgroLingua B.V., The Netherlands, 96 pp.

Nussbaumer, H.J., 1981. The Fast Fourier Transform. Fast Fourier Transform and Convolution Algorithms. Springer Series in Information Sciences, 2: 80-111. Springer, Berlin, Heidelberg. https://doi.org/10.1007/978-3-662-00551-4_4

Nuwer, M.R., Comi, G., Emerson, R., Fuglsang-Frederiksen, A., Guérit, J.-M., Hinrichs, H., Ikeda, A., Luccas, F.J.C. and Rappelsberger, P., 1998. IFCN standards for digital recording of clinical EEG. Electroencephalography and Clinical Neurophysiology, 106(3): 259-261. https://doi.org/10.1016/S0013-4694(97)00106-5

Olson, J.C. and Ray, W.J., 1983. Using Brain-Wave Measures to Assess Advertising Effects. Marketing Science Institute, Cambridge, MA, USA, 44 pp.

Orvis, G., 2016. The Science of Smell: How Retailers Can Use Scent Marketing to Influence Shoppers. Available at: https://www.shopify.com/retail/the-science-of-smell-how-retailers-can-use-scent-marketing-to-make-more-sales

Paluchová, J., Berčík, J. and Horská, E., 2017. The sense of smell. In: Sendra-Nadal, E. and Carbonell-Barrachina, A.Á. (eds) Sensory and aroma marketing. Wageningen Academic Publishers, Wageningen, the Netherlands, pp. 27-60. https://doi.org/10.3920/978-90-8686-841-4_2

Panovská, Z., Ilko, V. and Doležal, M., 2021. Air Quality as a Key Factor in the Aromatisation of Stores: A Systematic Literature Review. Applied Sciences, 11(16): 7697. https://doi.org/10.3390/app11167769

Parsons, A.G., 2009. Use of scent in a naturally odourless store. International Journal of Retail & Distribution Management, 37(5): 440-452. https://doi.org/10.1108/09590550910954928

Patel, N., 2021. The Psychology of Excitement: How to Better Engage Your Audience. HubSpot. Available at: https://blog.hubspot.com/marketing/psychology-of-excitement

Pavelka, A., 2017. Spotrebiteľská neuroveda ako moderný spôsob skúmania spotrebiteľského správania. Bachelor Thesis. SPU v Nitre, Nitra, Slovak Republic, 59 pp.

Pavelka, A., 2019. Elektroencefalografia, ako nástroj sledovania vplyvu aróm na emócie spotrebiteľov. Diploma Thesis. SPU v Nitre, Nitra, Slovak Republic, 93 pp.

Peck, J. and Shu, S.B., 2009. The Effect of Mere Touch on Perceived Ownership. Journal of Consumer Research, 36(3): 434-447. https://doi.org/10.1086/598614

Peck, J. and Wiggins, J., 2006. It just feels good: Customers' affective response to touch and its influence on persuasion. Journal of Marketing, 70(4): 56-69. https://doi.org/10.1509%2Fjmkg.70.4.056

Peck, J., Barger, V.A. and Webb, A., 2013. In search of a surrogate for touch: The effect of haptic imagery on perceived ownership. Journal of Consumer Psychology, 23(2): 189-196. https://doi.org/10.1016/j.jcps.2012.09.001

Plassmann, H., Venkatraman, V., Huettel, S. and Yoon, C., 2015. Consumer Neuroscience: Applications, Challenges, and Possible Solutions. Journal of Marketing Research, 52(4): 427-435. https://doi.org/10.1509/jmr.14.0048

Ramirez, R. and Vamvakousis, Z., 2012. Detecting Emotion from EEG Signals Using the Emotive EPOC Device. In Zanzotto, F.M., Tsumoto, S., Taatgen, N. and Yao, Y. (eds) Brain Informatics. BI 2012. Lecture Notes in Computer Science, 7670: 175-184. Springer. https://doi.org/10.1007/978-3-642-35139-6_17

REIMA AirConcept, 2019. AromaStreamer® 650 Bluetooth – Professional scent machine for rooms of approx. 150 m2. Available at: https://www.duftmarketing.de/en/productinfo/items/aromastreamer-650-bluetooth.html

Rich, B.A., Holroyd, T., Carver, F.W., Onelio, L.M., Mendoza, J.K., Cornwell, B.R., Fox, N.A., Pine, D.S., Coppola, R. and Leibenluft, E., 2010. A preliminary study of the neural mechanisms of frustration in pediatric bipolar disorder using magnetoencephalography. Depression and Anxiety, 27(3): 276-286. https://doi.org/10.1002/da.20649

Rimkute, J., Moraes, C. and Ferreira, C., 2015. The effects of scent on consumer behavior. International Journal of Consumer Studies, 40(1): 24-34. https://doi.org/10.1111/ijcs.12206

Rodas-Areiza, J.A. and Montoya-Restrepo, L., 2018. Methodological proposal for the analysis and measurement of sensory marketing integrated to the consumer experience. DYNA, 85(207): 54-59. ISSN 0012-7353. http://doi.org/10.15446/dyna.v85n207.71937

Rodrigues, C., Hultén, B. and Brito, C., 2011. Sensorial brand strategies for value co-creation. Innovative Marketing, 7(2): 40-47.

Roschk, H. and Hosseinpour, M., 2020. Pleasant Ambient Scents: A Meta-Analysis of Customer Responses and Situational Contingencies. Journal of Marketing, 84(1): 125-145. https://doi.org/10.1177/0022242919881137

Rothschild, M.L., Hyun, Y.J., Reeves, B., Thorson, E. and Goldstein, R., 1988. Hemispherically lateralized EEG as a response to television commercials. Journal of Consumer Research, 15(2): 185-198.

Sakamoto, R., Minoura, K., Usui, A., Ishizuka, Y. and Kanba, S., 2005. Effectiveness of Aroma on Work Efficiency: Lavender Aroma during Recesses Prevents Deterioration of Work Performance. Chemical Senses, 30(8): 683-691. https://doi.org/10.1093/chemse/bji061

Sayorwan, W., Siripornpanich, V., Piriyapunyaporn, T., Hongratanaworakit, T., Kotchabhakdi, N. and Ruangrungsi, N., 2012. The effects of lavender oil inhalation on emotional states, autonomic nervous system, and brain electrical activity. Journal of the Medical Association of Thailand = Chotmaihet thangphaet, 95(4): 598-606.

Scala, K., 2005. Scent Delivery Devices and Methods. United States Patent Application Publication. Publication number US 2006/0074742 A1, Application number: 11/234,202. Available at: http://www.faqs.org/patents/app/20080267833

Scent Company, 2019. Chasing Galeries Lafayette Katara Plaza perfume sillage. Available at: http://blog.scentcompany.info/galeries-lafayette-katara-plaza-scent-marketing/

Schifferstein, H.N.J. and Blok, S.T., 2002. The Signal Function of Thematically (In)congruent Ambient Scents in a Retail Environment. Chemical Senses, 27(6, July 2002): 539-549. https://doi.org/10.1093/chemse/27.6.539

Schiffman, L. and Wisenblit, J.L., 2019. Consumer Behavior. Pearson, New Jersey, USA, 512 pp.

Schwab, W., Davidovich-Rikanati, R. and Lewinsohn, E., 2008. Biosynthesis of plant-derived flavor compounds. The Plant Journal, 54(4): 712-732. https://doi.org/10.1111/j.1365-313x.2008.03446.x

Secundo, L. and Sobel, N., 2006. The Influence of Smelling Coffee on Olfactory Habituation. Chemical Senses, 31(5), A52.

Sellaro, R., van Dijk, W.W., Paccani, C.R., Hommel, B., & Colzato, L.S., 2015. A question of scent: lavender aroma promotes interpersonal trust. Frontiers in Psychology, 5: 1486. https://doi.org/10.3389/fpsyg.2014.01486

Serras, L., 2018. How Brands Benefit From Scent Marketing. Available at: https://www.packagingstrategies.com/articles/94740-how-brands-benefit-from-scent-marketing

Setzer W.N., 2009. Essential oils and anxiolytic aromatherapy. Natural Product Communications, 4(9): 1305-1316.

Shimmer, 2018. GSR+ User Guide Revision 1.13. Available at: http://www.shimmersensing.com/images/uploads/docs/GSR%2B_User_Guide_rev1.13.pdf

Shimmer, 2019a. Consensys ECG Development Kits. Available at: http://www.shimmersensing.com/products/ecg-development-kit

Shimmer, 2019b. Shimmer3 GSR+ Unit. Available at: http://www.shimmersensing.com/products/shimmer3-wireless-gsr-sensor#download-tab

Shu, S.B. and Peck, J., 2011. Psychological ownership and affective reaction: Emotional attachment process variables and the endowment effect. Journal of Consumer Psychology, 21 (4): 439-452. https://doi.org/10.1016/j.jcps.2011.01.002

Sowndhararajan, K. and Kim, S., 2016. Influence of Fragrances on Human Psychophysiological Activity: With Special Reference to Human Electroencephalographic Response. Scientia Pharmaceutica, 84(4): 724-751. https://doi.org/10.3390/scipharm84040724

Sowndhararajan, K., Cho, H., Yu, B. and Kim, S., 2015. Effect of olfactory stimulation of isomeric aroma compounds, (+)-limonene and terpinolene on human electroencephalographic activity. European Journal of Integrative Medicine, 7: 561-566. https://doi.org/10.1016/j.eujim.2015.08.006

Sowndhararajan, K., Seo, M., Kim, M., Kim, H. and Kim, S., 2017. Effect of essential oil and supercritical carbon dioxide extract from the root of Angelica gigas on human EEG activity. Complementary Therapies in Clinical Practice, 28: 161-168. https://doi.org/10.1016/j.ctcp.2017.05.010

Soyyilmaz, D. 2021. The Anatomy of an EEG Cap. Available at: https://imotions.com/blog/eeg-cap/

Spangenberg, E.R., Crowley, A.E. and Henderson, P.W., 1996. Improving the Store Environment: Do Olfactory Cues Affect Evaluations and Behaviors? Journal of Marketing, 60(2), 67-80. https://doi.org/10.1177/002224299606000205

Spence, C., Velasco, C. and Petit, O., 2019. The Consumer Neuroscience of Packaging. In: Velasco, C. and Spence, C. (eds) Multisensory Packaging. Palgrave Macmillan, pp. 319-347. https://doi.org/10.1007/978-3-319-94977-2_12

Srivastava, M. and Singh, G., 2011. Sensory Marketing in Retail: Why not all five? In: SIMSARC11 – SIMS Annual Research Conference – Big India Breaching Boundaries: India By 2020, pp. 74-78. Available at: https://www.researchgate.net/publication/299366291_Sensory_Marketing_in_Retail_Why_not_all_five

Statistics Solutions, 2019. Chi-Square Test of Independence. Available at: https://www.statisticssolutions.com/non-parametric-analysis-chi-square/

Statistics.com – The Institute for Statistics Education, 2020. Contingency Table. Available at: https://www.statistics.com/glossary/contingency-table/

Stikic, M., Berka, C., Levendowski, D.J., Rubio, R.F., Tan, V., Korszen, S., Douglas, B. and Wurzer, D., 2014. Modeling temporal sequences of cognitive state changes based on a combination of EEG-engagement, EEG-workload, and heart rate metrics. Frontiers in Neuroscience, 8: 342. https://doi.org/10.3389%2Ffnins.2014.00342

TCT – Trans Cranial Technologies, 2012. 10/20 System Positioning Manual. Trans Cranial Technologies, Wanchai, Hong Kong, 20 pp. Available at: https://www.trans-cranial.com/docs/10_20_pos_man_v1_0_pdf.pdf

The Aroma Trace, 2020. 10 examples of successful Olfactory Marketing. Available at: https://thearomatrace.com/best-examples-of-olfactory-marketing-in-companies/

Vlahos, J., 2007. Scent and sensibility. The New York Times. Available at: https://www.nytimes.com/2007/09/09/realestate/keymagazine/909SCENT-txt.html

Wansink, B., 2014. Slim by Design: Mindless Eating Solutions for Everyday Life. Harper Collins Publishers, New York, USA, 320 pp.

Yadava, M., Kumar, P., Saini, R., Roy, P.P., Dogry, D.P., 2017. Analysis of EEG signals and its application to neuromarketing. Multimedia Tools and Applications, 76(18): 19087-19111. ISSN 1573-7721. https://doi.org/10.1007/s11042-017-4580-6

Yavuz, E. and Aydemir, Ö., 2016. Olfaction Recognition by EEG Analysis Using Wavelet Transform Features. In: International Symposium on INnovations in Intelligent SysTems and Applications, pp. 1-4. https://doi.org/10.1109/INISTA.2016.7571827

Zhang, Z., Zhang, H., Li, X., Zhang, L. and Guan, C., 2017. Toward EEG-based Olfactory Sensing through Spatial Temporal Subspace Optimization. In: 2017 International Conference on Orange Technologies (ICOT), pp. 168-171. https://doi.org/10.1109/ICOT.2017.8336114

Zurawicki, L., 2010. Neuromarketing: Exploring the Brain of the Consumer. Springer-Verlag Berlin Heidelberg, Berlin, Germany, 273 pp.

Appendix A – Friedman test

Respondent	1. How do you evaluate Scent 1?	2. How do you evaluate Scent 2?	3. How do you evaluate Scent 3?
1	5	2	2
2	5	4	3
3	4	4	4
4	4	4	2
5	3	4	2
6	4	4	3
7	4	4	1
8	4	3	1
9	4	3	2
10	3	2	2
11	5	5	4
12	5	3	4
13	4	3	4
14	3	2	4
15	4	4	2
16	4	3	5
17	3	4	3
18	3	4	2
19	2	4	4
20	5	2	2
21	5	4	4
22	4	5	4

	Scent 1 evaluation processing	Scent 2 evaluation processing	Scent 3 evaluation processing	g_i	t_{ij}	t_{ij}^3	t_{ij}^{3-k}
1	3	1.5	1.5	2	2	8	5
2	3	2	1				
3	1	1	1	1	3	27	24
4	2.5	2.5	1	2	2	8	5
5	2	3	1				
6	2.5	2.5	1	2	2	8	5
7	2.5	2.5	1	2	2	8	5
8	3	2	1				
9	3	2	1				
10	3	1.5	1.5	2	2	8	5
11	2.5	2.5	1	2	2	8	5
12	3	1	2				
13	2.5	1	2.5	2	2	8	5
14	2	1	3				
15	2.5	2.5	1	2	2	8	5
16	2	1	3				
17	1.5	3	1.5	2	2	8	5
18	2	3	1				
19	1	2.5	2.5	2	2	8	5
20	3	1.5	1.5	2	2	8	5
21	3	1.5	1.5	2	2	8	5
22	1.5	3	1.5	2	2	8	5
R_{ij}	52	44	33				89
$(R_{ij}-n{\times}R_{ij})^2$	64	0	121				
SUM	185						
F*	10,114						
TH	5,991						

Appendix B – Chi-square independence test

Scent 1

	Empirical distribution			Theoretical distribution		
	Female	Male	Sum	Female	Male	Sum
Very unpleasant	2	4	6	3.0	3.0	6.0
Unpleasant	7	3	10	5.0	5.0	10.0
Neutral	2	3	5	2.5	2.5	5.0
Pleasant	0	1	1	0.5	0.5	1.0
Sum	11	11	22	11.0	11.0	22.0

	X^2		
	Female	Male	Sum
Very unpleasant	0.333	0.333	0.667
Unpleasant	0.800	0.800	1.600
Neutral	0.100	0.100	0.200
Pleasant	0.500	0.500	1.000
Sum	1.733	1.733	3.467
Test statistic			3.467
Critical value			7.815

Scent 2

	Empirical distribution			Theoretical distribution		
	Female	Male	Sum	Female	Male	Sum
Very unpleasant	1	1	2	1	1	2
Unpleasant	7	4	11	5.5	5.5	11
Neutral	2	3	5	2.5	2.5	5
Pleasant	1	3	4	2	2	4
Sum	11	11	22	11	11	22

X^2			
	Female	Male	Sum
Very unpleasant	0.000	0.000	0.000
Unpleasant	0.409	0.409	0.818
Neutral	0.100	0.100	0.200
Pleasant	0.500	0.500	1.000
Sum	1.009	1.009	2.018
Test statistic			2.018
Critical value			7.815

Scent 3

	Empirical distribution			Theoretical distribution		
	Female	Male	Sum	Female	Male	Sum
Very unpleasant	0	1	1	0.5	0.5	1
Unpleasant	3	5	8	4	4	8
Neutral	2	1	3	1.5	1.5	3
Pleasant	6	2	8	4	4	8
Sum	0	2	2	1	1	2

X^2			
	Female	Male	Sum
Very unpleasant	0.500	0.500	1.000
Unpleasant	0.250	0.250	0.500
Neutral	0.167	0.167	0.333
Pleasant	1.000	1.000	2.000
Sum	1.000	1.000	2.000
Test statistic			5.833
Critical value			9.488